the gospel
Framework

the gospel
Framework

fiction or fact?

A critical evaluation of
Der Rahmen der Geschichte Jesu
by Karl Ludwig Schmidt

DAVID R. HALL

paternoster
press

Copyright © David Hall 1998

First published 1998 by Paternoster Press

04 03 02 01 00 99 98   7 6 5 4 3 2 1

Paternoster Press is an imprint of Paternoster Publishing,
P.O. Box 300, Carlisle, Cumbria CA3 0QS

The right of David Hall to be identified as the Author of this Work has been
asserted by him in accordance with the Copyright, Designs and Patents Act 1988.

British Library Cataloguing in Publication Data

A catalogue record for this book is available from the British Library.

ISBN 0-85364-799-2

This book is printed using Suffolk Book paper which is 100% acid free.

Typeset by WestKey Ltd, Falmouth, Cornwall
Printed in Great Britain by Clays Ltd, St Ives plc

Contents

Introduction

Karl Ludwig Schmidt's book 'The Framework of the Story of Jesus' (*Der Rahmen der Geschichte Jesu*) is an astonishing achievement.[1] Written by a young man of twenty-eight years old, a teacher in the theological faculty at Berlin, it rapidly gained a reputation as a classic work of New Testament scholarship such as none of the author's other writings achieved. In the words of Stephen Neill, 'Schmidt continued to do valuable work in various directions. . . . But it was the first book which established his reputation; he never perhaps quite equalled again the brilliance and originality of his first notable contribution to theology.'[2]

In this book I shall attempt to evaluate one specific area of Schmidt's achievement. I shall not be concerned so much with the brilliance and originality of his work as with the more mundane matter of the logical force of his arguments. I propose to examine these arguments in some detail, and to ask whether they are logically valid and whether they prove the point he is trying to make. My conclusion is that most of his arguments are logically flawed and that his thesis therefore remains unproven.

At first sight it may seem strange to subject a book published nearly eighty years ago to this kind of scrutiny. Scholarship has moved on in the course of the twentieth century, and I doubt if any scholar today would wish to support Schmidt's views in every detail. Nevertheless, Schmidt's *Rahmen* is widely regarded today as an authoritative work, whose main thesis can safely be presupposed in scholarly research. It forms part of the foundation of modern study of the gospels, and therefore the question of its logical validity is still of the greatest importance.

In his book Schmidt analyses the framework of the synoptic gospels, with special emphasis on Mark. By 'framework' he means the introductory and concluding statements attached to the individual stories, which bind them together into a continuous narrative. He examines these statements one by one and concludes that they are historically worthless[3] – that Mark's information came to him in the form of isolated stories, that he had no idea how these stories were related to each other in time or locality, and that the framework that binds them together was an artificial construction of the evangelist.

Subsequent scholarship has largely endorsed Schmidt's judgment. Typical is the statement of W.G. Kümmel:

> Schmidt demonstrates that the classical two-source theory must be enlarged to include the insight that behind both sources, and behind our Gospels in general, stand individual reports orally transmitted, which the evangelists have linked together at secondhand without any knowledge of the historical connection in accordance with principles based on their content, or even on pragmatic grounds.[4]

In Kümmel's view, Schmidt prepared the way for Form Criticism and provided its logical basis:

> The way to form-critical research of the synoptic material was paved by K.L. Schmidt through his demonstration that in Mk the framework of the narrative was the creation of the author . . .[5]

and again:

> The form-critical method takes its departure from the fact demonstrated by K.L. Schmidt that the framework – i.e. the narrative material in the Synoptics which links together the individual accounts and sayings or groups of sayings – is secondary.[6]

This judgment is endorsed by Raymond F. Collins:

> 'Dibelius' general approach to the Synoptics was similar to that of Karl Ludwig Schmidt (1891–1956), whose 'The Framework of the Story of Jesus' (*Der Rahmen der Geschichte Jesu*) (1919) effectively demonstrated that the orally transmitted individual gospel stories had their life situation in the worship of the early Christian community, and that Mark, followed by the other Synoptists, had created the literary framework in which these Gospel traditions were preserved.[7]

In similar vein Norman Perrin declares:

> Schmidt concerned himself with the framework of the Gospel narratives, showing that this framework was normally supplied by the evangelist himself, who had taken small units of tradition and fitted them loosely together in accordance with his own interests and concerns.[8]

In his survey of a century of New Testament study John Riches underlines the significance of Schmidt's contribution:

> Schmidt's book . . . was restricted to a consideration of the framework which the evangelists had created for the stories and discourse material which they collected. What he showed convincingly was that this framework was a loosely constructed expedient by which the evangelist was able to draw together a mass of traditional material into a coherent narrative. It was, that is to say, an editorial device by means of which collectors of the tradition could arrange their material, not a reliable historical account of the outline of Jesus's life and death. Source criticism, by identifying Mark as the oldest Gospel, had led many to suppose that it was, therefore, a reliable source of information about the course of Jesus's life. Schmidt's work simply undermined such a view. The evangelists were collectors of folk-tales, not reporters of historical events.[9]

W.R. Telford also emphasizes the long-term influence of Schmidt's thesis in twentieth-century Markan studies:

> Schmidt (1919) drew attention to the "unit-structure" of the Gospel, the "pearls and string" pattern evident in its composition. He demonstrated that the Gospel consisted (with the exception of the longer passion narrative) of a whole series of separate and discrete units (pericopae) linked by a largely artificial and extremely loose overall geographical and chronological framework. This framework was for the most part the evangelist's own creation, as evidenced, among other things, by the freedom exhibited by Matthew and Luke in altering it. Much of the traditional material represented by these pericope-units exhibited a topical arrangement in the Gospel, but not one conditioned by historical actuality. This result, though subsequently qualified, has not been successfully overturned.[10]

The scholarly judgments just quoted agree on three points:

1   that the framework of Mark's gospel was largely an artificial construction of the evangelist with no historical basis.
2   that Schmidt has 'demonstrated' this fact. I take this to mean that he has provided logical arguments so convincing that an unbiased reader is bound to accept them.
3   that subsequent scholarship has rightly accepted this fact as a presupposition for further research.

The question I wish to raise is whether this confidence is justified – whether Schmidt has in fact 'demonstrated' his theory. I shall seek to show that there are serious logical deficiencies in the arguments Schmidt employs, and that his whole case rests on unsubstantiated presuppositions. If this is true, it raises some fundamental questions. If, as is widely believed, Schmidt's thesis provides a logical foundation not only for form-criticism but also for redaction-criticism and other later developments, then cracks in the foundation must call into question the research that has been built upon it. Moreover, the methods employed by Schmidt were not, in most cases, peculiar to him. They were used by scholars before him, and have been widely used throughout the twentieth century. Therefore this study of the methods of argument of one particular scholar may well serve as a case-study with wider implications.

Schmidt's technique can be compared to an artillery bombardment. His main objective is to demolish the historical credibility of the Markan framework. In this work of demolition he employs a number of arguments – some are like big guns, some are like small hand grenades. The deployment of all these weapons produces a cumulative effect – a kind of blitzkrieg – whose purpose is to shatter the Markan framework into pieces. Just as the effectiveness of an artillery bombardment depends ultimately on the effectiveness of individual shells, so also does the effectiveness of a cumulative argument depend on the effectiveness of the individual arguments of which it is composed.

When Schmidt's arguments are analysed, they can be divided into six main categories. In Part One (chapters 1–6) I propose to examine these categories one by one, and thus to make an overall assessment of the effectiveness of his arsenal of weapons. In Part Two (chapters 7–13) I shall look at seven gospel passages, on each of which Schmidt unleashes a variety of arguments from his arsenal, and thus assess the cumulative effect of such an assault. In chapter 14 I shall investigate the arms dealers who supplied Schmidt with his arsenal – the scholars who preceded him and inspired his methodology. In chapter 15 I shall consider the long-term effect of Schmidt's attempted demolition of the Markan framework on New Testament scholarship in the twentieth century, and suggest that an alternative strategy to saturation bombardment would have been more appropriate.

Many of the arguments employed by Schmidt are discussed in more general terms in my previous book *The Seven Pillories of Wisdom*, which considers seven types of argument commonly used in New Testament study. Readers desiring a more detailed analysis of these arguments should refer to that book, to which the present case-study is in some respects a follow-up.[11]

Notes

1 Karl Ludwig Schmidt, *Der Rahmen der Geschichte Jesu* (Trowitzsch & Son, Berlin, 1919)

2 Stephen Neill, *The Interpretation of the New Testament 1861–1961* (Oxford University Press, London 1966) 237.

3 The phrase 'historische Wertlosigkeit' occurs on p.17: 'It is illegitimate to proceed automatically from recognition of the historical worthlessness of the Markan outline to endorsement of the Johannine outline.'

4 Werner Georg Kümmel, *The New Testament: the History of the Investigation of its Problems* (tr. S. McLean Gilmour and Howard Clark Kee) (Abingdon Press 1972; SCM, London 1973) 328.

5 Werner Georg Kümmel, *Introduction to the New Testament* tr. Howard Clark Kee (Abingdon and SCM, London 1975) 50.

6 Ibid. 76.

7 Raymond F. Collins, *Introduction to the New Testament* (Doubleday, New York 1983) 62.

8 Norman Perrin, *What is Redaction Criticism?* (Fortress, Philadelphia and SPCK, London 1970) 15.

9 John K. Riches, *A Century of New Testament Study* (Lutterworth Press, Cambridge 1993) 51.

10 William R. Telford, *The Interpretation of Mark* (T and T. Clark, Edinburgh 1995[2]) 5.

11 David R. Hall, *The Seven Pillories of Wisdom* (Mercer University Press, Macon, Georgia 1990)

Part I

1

The Argument from Presuppositions

We begin our study of Schmidt's arguments by examining his presuppositions. This is appropriate because the argument from presuppositions is the fundamental argument underlying the whole book. Schmidt's method is simple. First he states as a fact an unproved theory for which he provides no evidence. Then he uses this theory as a basis for making literary judgments on specific passages. There are three theories in particular that are treated in this way.

i)   The theory of early church storytellers

A great deal of Mark's gospel consists of separate stories or 'pericopes' – miracle stories, parables and conversations. Mark's source for these stories, according to Schmidt, was a circle of story-tellers (*Erzähler-kreis*) who used to tell the stories of Jesus in the context of worship. The way they did this is graphically described in Schmidt's commentary on the opening words of Mark 1:4: ἐγένετο Ἰωάννης (John the Baptist came). He argues that in the tradition the story of John the Baptist began with the words καὶ ἐγένετο Ἰωάννης (*and* John came), and that Mark has omitted the word καί from his source because it did not fit in with the Old Testament quotation in the preceding verse. The reason for assuming the existence of this imaginary καί is the nature of the tradition. When the early Christians met together, the stories of Jesus used to be told by a storytellers' circle. When one story-teller had finished, another would continue with the words καὶ ἐγένετο (and it came to pass) and start to tell another story. In this way there arose complexes of stories, joined to each other, whether in oral or written form, with the word καί or its Aramaic equivalent. These stories, or complexes of stories, formed the raw material of the evangelist.[1]

In the middle of this description come the astonishing words: 'we don't know anything definite about these matters' (*wir wissen über diese Dinge nichts Bestimmtes*). In other words, the whole of this passage is an exercise in scholarly imagination with no factual basis. Schmidt then proceeds to justify his procedure. He asserts that anyone who tries to picture in his imagination the earliest period of gospel tradition must resort to hypothesis at this point, knowing that it cannot be developed into infallible proof, but that nevertheless it helps us to see things, at least in general terms, in their correct historical light.[2]

There are two problems with this procedure. The first is that oral tradition can function in many different ways, and Schmidt's reconstruction can at best be only one possibility out of many. Kenneth Bailey, writing out of many years' experience of hearing stories told in the Middle East, has distinguished three main ways in which oral traditions are transmitted. 'Formal controlled oral tradition' involves the formal transfer of tradition from teacher to pupil, in the manner envisaged for the gospel tradition by Riesenfeld and Gerhardsson and practised today by those who learn by heart the Qur'an and other Arabic texts. 'Informal uncontrolled oral tradition' has no formal structure of teacher and pupil, everyone being free to add or subtract as the stories are passed on, in the way that rumours or atrocity stories are passed on today. 'Informal controlled oral tradition' functions in the setting of a community gathering at which the elders recite traditional stories, poetry, proverbs etc. The informal control is exercised by the members of the community, to whom the material is familiar, and who will be quick to point out any deviation from the accepted form. In the case of poems and proverbs, no deviation at all is acceptable. In the case of stories, the main plot and punch-line must not change, but a degree of improvisation is allowed in the details. It is this model that Bailey thinks to be most helpful for understanding the gospel tradition.[3]

Schmidt believes in some form of controlled tradition so far as the passion narrative is concerned. He thinks that the form of the passion narrative was fixed very early. One of its striking features was the silence of Jesus. Later on, people would probably have liked to attribute to Jesus words of defence against Pilate and the Sanhedrin, but in Schmidt's opinion this was not possible because 'the account had already for some time had a fixed form and could no longer be altered without damage to the settled mind of the community.'[4] However, Schmidt does not believe in the same degree of community control with regard to the rest of the tradition, which he describes as 'a tradition with various strata, brought to birth from a variety of interests and split into a mass of separate stories'.[5] In other words, it is what Bailey would call 'informal uncontrolled oral tradition'.

This contrast between strict community control of the passion narrative and the uncontrolled nature of the rest of the tradition seems to Schmidt to have a parallel in the traditions of the early martyrs. Accounts of the death of the martyrs attained a fixed form at an early stage, whereas the legends about their life and work that developed later included a lot of historically doubtful material.[6] But this parallel has a limited value. Jesus was not only a martyr, he was a teacher and a prophet.[7] C.H. Dodd has drawn attention to the continuity between the gospels and the portrayal of the early kerygma in Acts, where Jesus appears not only as a dying and rising saviour but also as a prophet mighty in word and deed.[8] For example, in Peter's summary of the kerygma in Acts 10: 34–43, the death of Jesus is described in six words out of a total of 178, and the healing ministry of Jesus is described in much greater detail. Moreover, Jesus was the founder of the community, whose words and actions created its community identity and would be treasured for that reason. Bailey describes how the Protestant churches in the south of Egypt treasure the stories of their founder John Hogg. He records a pronouncement story relating to Hogg that ends with an Arabic punch-line, and states his confidence that this Arabic sentence is a record of Hogg's exact words spoken over a hundred years before and never previously written down.[9]

It is impossible to say how far oral tradition in the churches of Mark's day followed the pattern of the Middle Eastern communities familiar to Bailey. What one can say with confidence is that oral tradition operates in a variety of ways. Schmidt's limitation of the operation of controlled tradition to the passion narrative alone, and his belief in the uncontrolled nature of the rest of the tradition, do not constitute the only possible hypothesis.

The second, even more serious, weakness in Schmidt's procedure is his almost total neglect of the role of eyewitnesses. According to the early church Fathers Mark was the apostle Peter's interpreter and his gospel was largely based on what Peter had taught. Our earliest source for this tradition, Bishop Papias, flourished in the first half of the

second century and claimed to have been in contact with those who
had heard the teaching of the apostles.[10] The Papias tradition suggests
that the church to which Mark belonged heard the stories of Jesus not
only from storytellers but also from the lips of Peter. As this tradition
goes against Schmidt's presuppositions, he simply ignores it, and
treats his own imaginative reconstruction as if it were the only one
available.

I have discovered only two incidental references to the external
evidence in Schmidt's book. The first is in a footnote approving
Johannes Weiss's judgment, in the light of 'the well-known Papias
reference to Mark', that old Petrine traditions lie behind Mark 1:16ff.
and 1:20ff.[11] What Schmidt seems to mean by 'old Petrine traditions'
is that words originally spoken by Peter had eventually reached Mark
after passing through the lips of various storytellers in the process.
This is a far cry from what Papias believed.

The other reference is to the presence in the Capernaum stories
and some Sea of Galilee stories of precise scenic details such as are
absent elsewhere. These stories, Schmidt declares, play a special role
within the older Jesus-tradition, and make attractive the tradition
linking Mark with Capernaum and with Simon Peter. He suggests
that, whereas other stories about Jesus had lost all geographical detail,
this process was delayed in the case of the Capernaum and Sea of
Galilee stories: these stories do preserve fragments of an itinerary,
though the necessity for Mark to introduce other material of a
different type made a proper itinerary impossible.[12]

It is not clear how this statement can be reconciled with Schmidt's
earlier declaration that the stories of Jesus were transmitted through
a circle of storytellers. His allusion to the special role of the Capernaum and Sea of Galilee stories could mean that in their case the
general statements made earlier about the transmission of the tradition do not necessarily apply. More probably, he means that these
stories came to Mark through the mediation of the storytellers in the
normal manner, but where Peter was the original authority the
tradition in some undefined way operated differently. At any rate, the
possibility of *direct* contact between Mark and Peter, of the sort
envisaged by Papias and the early church fathers, is never considered
by Schmidt, whether in discussion of the Capernaum and Sea of
Galilee stories or elsewhere. It is not that he examines the early church
tradition and gives reasons for its rejection. He simply treats it as
unworthy of serious consideration.

There is, to be sure, a certain logic in this procedure. Schmidt believes that he has been *forced* into holding his presuppositions by his literary analysis, and that all sensible readers will be forced into the same conclusion as himself.[13] If the logical force of the analysis is indeed as strong as Schmidt claims, then external evidence becomes irrelevant – even if Papias had received his information from the lips of Mark himself we should be compelled to reject it. But if Schmidt's analysis does not have the logical force he claims – if it consists simply in putting forward one possible explanation of a set of complex phenomena, then the external evidence becomes an important factor in weighing one possibility against another.

Schmidt's approach to external evidence has been widely followed in the twentieth century. A remark of Vernon K. Robbins illustrates the persistence of this attitude. In compiling a list of the strengths of form criticism Robbins includes: 'an unwillingness to impose extrinsic data about authors into the intrinsic data in a New Testament document.'[14] The implication seems to be that any attempt to interpret the New Testament in the light of the external evidence is to be avoided on principle as a methodological weakness. In view of the wide prevalence of this attitude, it is not surprising that in Markan studies, in the words of W.R. Telford, 'while the traditional view still has its defenders (e.g. M. Hengel, 1985; B. Orchard, 1992) a direct and uniform Petrine connection has not in practice been a basic premise of most of the studies appearing in the 1960s onwards.'[15]

At the colloquy on the gospels held at San Antonio in 1977 one of the speakers was George Kennedy, Paddison Professor of Classics at the University of North Carolina. He concentrated on the external evidence for the gospels and particularly on Papias. When some participants expressed reservations about this concentration on external evidence, he insisted that classical scholars, when dealing with any piece of ancient literature, would normally go to the external evidence first, before resorting to modern methods of text analysis.[16] What Kennedy describes as the standard approach of classical scholars to an ancient text is diametrically opposed to the approach of Schmidt and of those scholars who share his methodology. If a cavalier attitude to external evidence is one of the characteristics that identify New Testament scholars as a distinct species in the world of scholarship, Schmidt must be given his share of the credit for this.

ii) The theory of travelling introductions

Schmidt believed that the circle of storytellers was not at all interested in the original context of the stories.[17] However, he also believed that many of these stories began with chronological or topographical introductions, which Mark has faithfully reproduced in his gospel. He reconciled these two beliefs by means of what we may call the theory of travelling introductions. This theory, which is presented as a fact (*Tatsache*), states that when the stories travelled from church to church there were fixed introductions that travelled with them.[18] Thus a story might begin with the words, 'After these things Jesus went to Capernaum.' According to Schmidt's theory words such as these would travel with the story wherever it went and in whatever context it was told. Mark would then take the story with its fixed introduction and place it in his gospel at an appropriate point. An uninitiated reader might think that the words 'after these things' meant 'after the events just recorded in the gospel', not realising that the words were a meaningless formula that Mark reproduced word for word because it was a fixed element in the story.

According to Schmidt some stories travelled around with introductions and others without, and Mark recorded them as they stood in either case. 'He reproduces the tradition handed down to him irrespective of whether it is localised or not. This unliterary procedure is his literary characteristic.'[19] Thus the theory of travelling introductions is Schmidt's way of explaining the variety of Mark's gospel, the presence of details of time and place in some pericopes such as are absent in others. In each case Mark was simply recording what he had received.

Schmidt does not explain why storytellers who were not interested in context should go on repeating parrot-fashion introductions that implied a context. His concern is not to justify his theory but to apply it. Whenever in Mark's gospel an introductory statement is attributed to tradition, it can be presumed on the basis of this theory to be out of context.

Let us look at some examples. In Mark 4 there are two references to a boat – the boat from which Jesus preached (v.1) and the boat in which he crossed the lake with his disciples (vv.35f.). Previous scholars had believed that this linkage went back to reminiscence of the actual sequence of events. Schmidt castigates Wellhausen and J. Weiss for arguing that some of the details about boats or about the time of day could be historical. They do not realize, he declares, that these are merely bits of framework which Mark took over from the tradition more or less blindly (*ziemlich unbesehen*).[20] The two possible explanations for the linkage of these stories that he takes seriously both preclude the idea of genuine reminiscence. If the two stories were already linked in the tradition, the unreliability of this linkage can be proved by recourse to the theory of travelling introductions. In Schmidt's words, 'stories of this sort travelled around along with their introductions and were given a new context without any alteration of their framework.' If, on the other hand, the linkage was created by Mark, this means that he discovered the story of the stilling of the storm (4:35–41) as a 'wandering story' (*Wandergeschichte*) and attached it to the story of Jesus preaching from a boat by the seashore because it seemed an appropriate place. In either case, we need not assume a genuine chronological connection because 'the essential thing is to understand the story as a single self-contained pericope. Viewed from this angle, a genuine historical connection can be seen to be something fortuitous, something secondary.'[21] Schmidt could hardly make it clearer that the basis of his judgment is his presuppositions – that early church storytellers told single isolated stories without any knowledge of their context, that they habitually prefaced these stories with introductions that falsely implied a context, and that Mark took over these introductions word for word and found for them the best context he could.

A further example of Schmidt's use of this theory is his treatment of the cursing of the fig-tree in Mark 11. According to Mark Jesus left Jerusalem for Bethany after his triumphal entry. Then (v.12) on the next day, after they left Bethany, he felt hungry, saw a barren fig-tree and cursed it. What is the source of the phrases 'on the next day' and 'after they left Bethany'? According to Schmidt it is possible that Bethany was named in the tradition and that the fig-tree story was already linked there with the story of the triumphal entry. But it is better to assume the existence of separate traditions which Mark has combined. He therefore suggests the following analysis: the fig-tree story originally began simply with the words 'on the next day'. He comments that introductory statements of this kind often travelled around with the stories to which they were attached, and that it was not Mark's custom to add such chronological statements on his own initiative. But it is Mark who has added the reference to Bethany. He wished to locate the story at this point in his narrative because the cursing of the fig-tree seemed appropriate to the mood of impending catastrophe. Since the story as he received it began with the words 'on the next day', and the previous story of the triumphal entry ended with a departure to Bethany in the evening (v.11), Mark related the two stories to each other by adding a reference to Bethany in v.12.[22]

The striking thing about this reconstruction is the complete lack of any evidence to support it. Whatever theological difficulties the fig-tree story may present, the statements of time and place in v.12 read perfectly naturally. Schmidt's reconstruction depends entirely on presupposition: the 'next day' cannot be a Markan addition because it is not typical of his style; and it cannot be historically accurate because, according to the travelling framework theory, all such introductory statements in the tradition are automatically out of context.[23]

The same point is illustrated in Schmidt's discussion of Mark 9:2, where Jesus took three disciples up the mount of transfiguration 'after six days'. Such a precise time statement is not typical of Mark and therefore in Schmidt's opinion must come from the tradition. Since the transfiguration story follows on smoothly from the preceding section, most scholars in Schmidt's day believed that the pericopes had belonged together in the tradition from the beginning. But Schmidt objects to this. The reason for his objection is not the possible symbolism linking the number 6 to the creation story (which he thinks would not have been important for Mark) but his general belief in the unhistorical nature of all such statements in the tradition:

> If Mark had discovered this transfiguration story along with its time-statement in a different context or as an isolated pericope, he could simply have inserted it here as it stood, since he paid no attention to matters of chronology. The words 'after six days' were for him simply a transition formula, and in this respect he saw things more correctly than the modern expositors who find here a graphic statement of time.

Accordingly Schmidt declares that the words 'after six days' do not constitute a concrete statement of time that goes back to the precise recollection of an eyewitness.[24]

This argument is a good example of Schmidt's scholarly method. He begins with a statement of possibility – Mark *could* have taken over the transfiguration story as an isolated pericope and placed it in a new context. But he ends with a statement of fact – the words 'after six days' *are not* based on the recollections of eyewitnesses. At first sight the statement that Mark *could* have transposed the story to a new context implies that the converse is also true: he could equally have found it already connected to the previous story in the tradition. But one can understand why Schmidt refuses to take seriously this latter possibility. To admit that a time-statement in the tradition could be correct in one instance would be the thin end of the wedge. It would mean that the same possibility would have to reckoned with in other cases also, and the assumption that all introductory statements in the tradition are historically worthless would have to be reconsidered.

The theory of travelling introductions is both dogmatic and flexible. It is dogmatic in the sense that the storytellers are credited with a uniform and invariable lack of interest in the original historical circumstances, so that the possibility that any introductory material in the tradition might be based on reminiscence is excluded on principle. It is flexible in the sense that the travelling introductions could take many forms, so that any introductory material in Mark that is credited to tradition, whatever its form, can come under the umbrella of the theory. In his commentary on the section of Mark's gospel from 2:1 to 3:6 Schmidt observes how varied are the frameworks of the stories in this section: some are localized, with vivid details; others are vague. He sees this as a consequence of the anecdotal character of these stories. The storytellers had basically no interest in their framework and this explains the variety. The vivid details are described as embellishments (*Rankenwerk*) which have been preserved 'more or less by chance'.[25] Presumably this means that some storytellers added more embellishments than others, so the degree of embellishment of a story depended on the chance of which storyteller happened to have told it.

The advantage of this reconstruction is that, whatever form a Markan introductory statement takes, it can be shown to be unhistorical. If the introduction to a story contains a lot of detail, this shows that the storyteller at some stage included (or invented) these details; if the introduction to a story contains little or no detail, this shows that the storyteller concerned had omitted the details. There is thus no type of framework in Mark that could possibly conflict with Schmidt's thesis.

A thesis of this kind cannot be proved or disproved. Since the storytellers are figments of Schmidt's imagination, he is free, like any other writer of fiction, to attribute to them any procedure he wishes. However, one cannot help wondering whether any group of people could show such a consistent lack of interest in the historical facts as

these hypothetical storytellers are alleged to have shown. Was there
not even one early church story-teller who occasionally wondered
when or where a particular incident took place and broke the pattern
of monolithic indifference?

iii)   The theory of Markan artlessness

The third cornerstone of Schmidt's thesis is his estimate of Mark as
an unsophisticated redactor rather than a creative author. Two of his
favourites descriptions of Mark's style are '*naiv*' (simple, unsophisticated) and '*ohne Kunst*' (artless). He quotes with approval
Schweitzer's judgment that Mark is lacking in both logic and psychology: Mark does not trace any development in Jesus, in the disciples
or in the external circumstances; nor does he provide any psychological motivation to link together the various events. Instead, he records
a series of events one after another without comment.[26]
  Schmidt does not regard this as a totally bad procedure. For
example, when relating the story of the rich young ruler, Luke differs
from Mark in stating at the beginning of the story that the man is a
leader in the community. Schmidt comments that the older, less
sophisticated tradition represented by Mark lets the character of a
person emerge gradually from the story itself.[27] There is a similar
contrast between Luke and Mark in their depiction of the teaching of
John the Baptist. Both gospels relate two elements in John's teaching
– the message of repentance and the coming Messiah. In Luke's case,
he first summarizes John's teaching on repentance and then describes
the popular debate as to whether John might be the Messiah which
led John to point away from himself to the one coming after him.
Schmidt contrasts this presentation with the unsophisticated style of
Mark and Matthew, who simply place the two elements in John's
preaching side by side without comment.[28] In both these cases Mark's
lack of sophistication appears almost as a virtue, in comparison with
the literary style of Luke.
  More commonly, however, Schmidt regards Mark's artlessness as
a negative feature, which leads him to attribute any evidence of artistry
in Mark not to the author but to the tradition. For instance, Mark 1:9
reads: 'And it came to pass in those days that Jesus came from
Nazareth and was baptized by John in the Jordan.' Schmidt argues

that the opening words of this verse must come from the tradition, on the grounds that Mark (unlike Matthew the Hebraizer) does not use the word ἐγένετο (it came to pass) in this construction elsewhere. The idea that Mark might have used the construction with ἐγένετο deliberately in order to emphasize the importance of the first appearance of Jesus is rejected because 'Mark is not such a deep thinker as that' (*so stark reflektierend ist aber Mk nicht*). In other words, Mark is so unsophisticated that the use of a solemn formula for a solemn occasion must be presumed to be beyond him.[29]

Schmidt makes a similar judgment in commenting on Mark's account of the death of John the Baptist (6:14–29). This account presents a difficulty for the theory of Markan artlessness. On the face of it Mark is using the flashback technique, widely used today in books and films. According to Mark (1:14) John's arrest preceded the Galilee ministry, so the account of that arrest in 6:17 belongs chronologically to chapter 1. The flashback as a literary technique would be beyond the scope of an artless author such as Schmidt believes Mark to have been. He therefore quotes (with apparent approval) the comment of Klostermann: 'here begins the great parenthesis in which all the verbs logically (though not perhaps in the mind of the unsophisticated storyteller) have the force of a pluperfect.' The implication is that Mark probably placed the account of the arrest and execution of John the Baptist in Chapter 6 without being sophisticated enough to realise that it was chronologically out of order.[30]

The main practical benefit to Schmidt's thesis of his low estimate of Mark's ability is that it explains Mark's mechanical use of his sources. According to Schmidt's theory, Mark faithfully reproduced the meaningless statements of time and place with which the storytellers began their stories, and adjusted them as best he could to the context in which he placed them. Such statements were reproduced artlessly because they were regarded merely as a means of linking one passage with another and the context was not seen as important. Schmidt describes Mark as 'on the whole only a compiler' (*im ganzen nur Kompilator*)[31] who was not interested in topography or chronology: 'The technique of the evangelist is manifest: he puts the stories side by side, in the form in which they have been handed down to him, and refuses to add topographical and chronological link-words on his own initiative.'[32]

In this respect Schmidt contrasts Mark with Matthew, and above all with Luke, who 'are not mere redactors but also to a certain extent authors'.[33]

In Schmidt's view the tradition is like a collection of pictures, some framed, some unframed; some stories containing statements of time and place, some without any; and the compilers of these stories, such as Mark, simply reproduced what they found and did not on the whole make sweeping changes.[34] In another place he compares the stories in Mark to a collection of pearls, and argues that we should not think of these pearls as forming a chain (loosely attached, so that Matthew and Luke could easily attach new pearls here and there), but rather as a disorganized heap (except for the rare cases in which groups of pearls were already attached to each other in the tradition).[35] It is on this almost totally negative view of Mark's literary ability that Schmidt's thesis depends.

What is the reason for this negative view? Schmidt himself believed that his estimate of Mark had been forced on him by the logic of his literary-critical methodology.[36] But our analysis of his book will reveal too many examples of forced exegesis and reliance on unproved presuppositions for this to be a total explanation. Rather, we should note that Schmidt's attitude was shared by many scholars of his day. I shall attempt an explanation of this phenomenon later;[37] for the moment let us simply take note of its existence.

iv) Practical application

Armed with these presuppositions, Schmidt then proceeds to analyse in detail the framework of each gospel pericope – the statements of time, place etc. that introduce and conclude the various gospel stories. There are two stages in this analysis. First, he divides the framework into fragments and assigns each fragment to one of four categories; and then he assesses the historicity of these fragments in the light of his classification. The four categories are as follows:

(i)   Introductory material that Mark found in his source at the beginning of a pericope.

(ii) Concluding material that Mark found in his source at the end of a pericope.

(iii) Connecting material that Mark found in his source in those relatively few cases in which two or more stories were already combined in the tradition.

(iv) Material added by Mark to enable what were originally separate pericopes to hang together in a connected narrative.

Though the classification of the various fragments of the framework takes up a good deal of space in Schmidt's book, there are two factors which indicate that classification was not his major concern. On the one hand, he is well aware of the tentative nature of such classification and on many occasions returns a verdict of 'not proven'. On the other hand, this uncertainty does not affect the main thrust of his argument. His aim is to prove that the framework material is unhistorical, and this he is able to do by appealing to his presuppositions, irrespective of the category to which any particular piece of the framework is assigned. Classification merely indicates which specific type of historical unreliability each piece of the framework should be found guilty of.

Schmidt recognizes, in particular, the inevitable uncertainty in deciding between category (iv) (material added by Mark) on the one hand and categories (i) to (iii) (material taken from the tradition) on the other hand. He quotes the views of two earlier scholars, J. Wellhausen and J. Weiss, on Mark's account of the stilling of the storm (4:35–41). Both scholars attribute some features of the story to tradition and some to Mark; but what Wellhausen attributes to Mark Weiss regards as traditional and vice versa. Schmidt comments that both scholars are indulging in '*Impressionismus*', and that a comparison of their varied opinions suggests that we should be cautious in dividing up the material into tradition and redaction.[38]

Even if a piece of framework is assigned to tradition the uncertainties remain. For example, Mark 7:31 states that Jesus left Tyre and travelled via Sidon and Decapolis to the Sea of Galilee. This verse is sandwiched between the story of the Syrophoenician woman(7:24–30) and the healing of the deaf and dumb man (7:32–37). Schmidt is unwilling to assign this verse to category (iv) (Markan additions), on the grounds that such additions are not usually as circumstantial as this. The verse is equally appropriate either as a conclusion to the earlier story or as an introduction to the later story. So Schmidt offers two possibilities. Either the verse belongs to category (iii) and the two stories were already linked in the tradition; or it is a combination of (i) and (ii)–a conclusion and introduction at the same time, which Mark has somehow or other remodelled into its present form.[39]

A similar situation arises with the statement in Mark 6:6 that Jesus toured the surrounding villages teaching. This statement immediately follows the account of Jesus's rejection at Nazareth and immediately precedes the sending out of the twelve on mission. Most previous scholars had treated it as an introduction to the following story, composed by Mark, even though the language is not particularly Markan. But Schmidt considers also both the possibility that it is an isolated short summary statement by Mark and the possibility that it belonged originally to the preceding story as a conclusion. He comments that it is often a matter of taste whether scholars regard such phrases as introductory or conclusory, and that it is often impossible to tell how far such summary statements are the work of the evangelist and how far they originally belonged to the preceding story.[40]

Schmidt then proceeds to make a comment that reveals why this uncertainty does not worry him. Statements such as the one in Mark 6:6, he declares, whether they were attached to the end of a story in the tradition or whether they were developed by Mark, were in either case never intended to be significant statements of topography or chronology in the development of a life of Jesus.[41] In other words, the question of historicity does not depend on the correctness of the classification. A piece of framework attached to a story in the tradition is bound to be unhistorical because the theory of travelling introductions (extended to cover also travelling conclusions) requires it to be so. A piece of framework added by Mark is also bound to be unhistorical because Mark had no interest in topography or chronology and no sources apart from the storytellers. Lack of historicity is determined not by classification but by presupposition.

Conclusion

In this chapter we have considered the presuppositions that underlie Schmidt's presentation, on the basis of which he is able to argue that all the framework material in Mark, whatever its form, is unhistorical. It is important to note, however, that his scepticism about the historicity of the framework does not extend to the narratives themselves. He seems to regard the introductions and conclusions to the gospel pericopes as similar to barnacles, which attach themselves to ships without necessarily making unseaworthy the vessels to which they cling. Again and again he declares his agnosticism as to whether a particular story is historical or unhistorical. For example, when discussing Mark 4 he warns against the casting of premature verdicts that the material is 'impossible' or 'psychologically incomprehensible'. He supports the protest of P. Fiebig and others against Jülicher's rule that Jesus never used allegory, and regards Wrede's picture of Jesus as too one-sided in failing to recognize the tensions Jesus felt. In his opinion previous scholars had allowed their literary judgment to be influenced in an unjustified manner by dubious assumptions about historicity.[42] For Schmidt the foundation of Gospel study is literary analysis. It is on this analysis that he concentrates, and it is the tools he uses in this analysis that we shall be examining in the next five chapters.

Notes

1   *Rahmen* 19. Schmidt's reconstruction has a doubtful grammatical base. The word ἐγένετο can have several meanings. Sometimes it is equivalent to the Hebrew wayy'hi (and it came to pass), where ἐγένετο introduces another verb that indicates what it was that came to pass (e.g. Matt. 7:28; Mark 1:9). On other occasions it means 'to come, to appear' (e.g. Luke 1:44; 6:13). Schmidt attributes to the storytellers regular use of the word in the former sense. But in Mark 1:4 it is used in the latter sense, and this verse is therefore not a proper illustration of the supposed practice of the storytellers. A similar failure to distinguish between the various meanings of ἐγένετο led to the mistranslation of Luke 2:2 in the New English Bible, where a single occurrence of ἐγένετο is translated both as 'was' and as 'took place'.

2   *Rahmen* 19.

3   Kenneth E. Bailey, 'Informal controlled oral tradition and the Synoptic Gospels', *Asia Journal of Theology* 5 (1991) 34–54, reprinted in *Themelios* Vol. 20 No. 2 (Jan. 95) 4–11. Bailey's 'informal controlled oral tradition' is similar to the idea of 'flexible transmission within fixed limits' which many scholars, following the researches of anthropologists such as A.B. Lord, regard as a better model for the gospel tradition than classical form criticism. See C.L. Blomberg's article 'Form Criticism' in Joel B. Green et al. (ed.) *A Dictionary of Jesus and the Gospels*, (Downers Grove, Illinois and IVP, Leicester 1992) 247.

4   *Rahmen* 306.

5   Ibid. 305.

6   Ibid. 305.

7   cf. Rainer Riesner, 'Jesus als Lehrer', *WUNT* 2.7 (Tübingen, Mohr 1981) and idem, 'Jüdische Elementarbildung und Evangelien-überlieferung', R.T. France & David Wenham (ed) *Gospel Perspectives* (JSOT, Sheffield) Vol. I, 209–223. Riesner emphasizes the importance of rote memorization in the three main places of education for Jewish boys – the home, the synagogue and the elementary school and points out how much of the teaching of Jesus is cast in an easily memorable form.

8   Charles Harold Dodd, *The Apostolic Preaching and its Development* (London, Hodder and Stoughton 1936).

9   Bailey, *Tradition* (Themelios edition) 8.

10   For a more detailed discussion of the Papias tradition see below pp. 164–173.
11   *Rahmen* 67 n. 2.
12   Ibid. 127.
13   In page v of the introduction to *Rahmen* Schmidt portrays the earliest Jesus-tra-
      dition as consisting in isolated pericopes, which were handed down for the most
      part without any firm indication of time or place, so that the topographical and
      chronological statements attached to the stories are in most cases simply a
      framework, like a frame added to a picture. He describes this as 'a basic
      methodical premiss which has been forced upon me by my analysis of the
      Synoptic Gospels'. (*Ein solcher methodologischer Grundgedanke, der sich mir aus
      der Analyse der Synoptiker aufgedrängt hat . . .*)
14   Vernon K. Robbins, 'Form Criticism (NT)' in D.N. Freedman (ed) *The Anchor
      Bible Dictionary* (NY, Doubleday 1992) II 843.
15   W.R. Telford, *Interpretation*, 2.
16   George Kennedy, 'Classical and Christian Source Criticism' in William O.
      Walker (ed) *The Relationship among the Gospels* (San Antonio TX: Trinity
      University Press 1978) 125–155. The comparison between the methods of
      classical and New Testament scholars comes in the ensuing discussion pp. 177f.
17   *Rahmen* VI: 'Those who told and handed down the stories of Jesus in the earliest
      period paid little or no attention to their context. Their sole interest was in the
      individual pericopes as illustrative material for use in Christian worship.'
18   Ibid: 'The fact that the introductions to the narratives are remarkably varied,
      and that they travelled around with the individual stories without any consid-
      eration of their proper context in the sequence of events, demonstrates again
      and again the "framework" character of this tradition.'
19   *Rahmen* 52.
20   Ibid. 137 n.1: 'Even scholars who, in general terms, correctly recognize the
      nature of Mark's gospel as a compilation continue to be influenced by the idea
      of a supposed chronology within this gospel. They do not realize that what we
      have here are pieces of framework which, precisely because they were only
      framework, were taken over from the tradition more or less blindly. And if a
      piece of framework was missing, that didn't matter.'
21   Ibid. 136f.
22   Ibid. 299f.
23   For discussion of Schmidt's treatment of the difference in chronology between
      Mark and Matthew see below pp. 71f.
24   *Rahmen* 222f.
25   Ibid. 103f: 'The framework material, insofar as it exists, takes many forms.
      Sometimes we have a localization combined with vivid details, sometimes the
      historical framework is completely vague. This variety is typical of such stories,
      which in some respects have a strongly anecdotal character. It is more or less by
      chance that the embellishments of these anecdotes have been preserved for us.
      The people who told and transmitted all these stories basically paid little
      attention to their framework. That is the reason for the variety.'
26   Ibid. VII.
27   Ibid. 242.
28   Ibid. 27.
29   Ibid. 29 and esp. n.1. It is interesting that, of the six occasions when Matthew
      uses ἐγένετο with an indicative verb to follow, five are a repetition of the same

formula (and it came to pass after Jesus had completed this teaching . . . 7:28; 11:1; 13:53; 19:1; 26:1).

30 Ibid. 175.
31 Ibid. 209: 'These separate pericopes have a great many topographical and chronological statements as a framework. But these are all put together side by side in an artless manner because these statements were only valued as transition markers. . . . An author who had composed these stories himself would have produced a much more simple and consistent topography. In practice the evangelist, who is on the whole only a compiler, has here taken over these things as they were handed down in the tradition and attached no value to them.'
32 Ibid. 67f.
33 Ibid. 68.
34 Ibid. 152.
35 Ibid. 281.
36 Ibid. V, quoted in note 13 above.
37 See Chapter 15 pp. 165f.
38 *Rahmen* 137 n.1: 'At this point scholars seem to me to be indulging in a kind of impressionism which certainly has some advantages. It creates the strength and freshness of Wellhausen's presentation in particular. But study of the varied opinions of those who share in this task warns us to be cautious in dividing the material between the tradition and the editorial work of the evangelist.'
39 Ibid. 200f.
40 Ibid. 160: 'The judgment as to what is regarded as introduction and what is regarded as conclusion is often a matter of taste. This can be seen from the variety of such judgments in both ancient and modern times. We have come across the same uncertainty in respect of 1:20f.; 1:39f.; 2:12f. and 3:6f. There is also another point: there is no way of telling how far all the summary statements are really a product of the work of the evangelist.'
41 Ibid.
42 Ibid. 132: 'One final point: in dealing with a tradition of this sort that is richer than we think, one should beware of premature verdicts such as "impossible", "psychologically incomprehensible", "unhistorical" . . . . The question of the historicity of the tradition, which has thus in important respects not been correctly answered, has influenced the literary treatment of the gospels in an unjustified manner. People have tried to manufacture the original connection of events as if all that was needed was a set formula.'

2

The Argument from Design

The argument from design is of great importance to Schmidt.[1] It consists in deciding what were the aims of each evangelist and then working out how specific elements in his gospel were composed in the light of these aims. This argument is of less importance in the consideration of Matthew's gospel, since in Schmidt's opinion Matthew was concerned with the use of the stories and teaching of Jesus in worship rather than with presenting any particular point of view.[2] The argument is, however, very significant in the analysis of Mark and Luke, and we shall consider these in turn.

i) Design in Mark

According to Schmidt one of the characteristics of Mark's style is 'Schematismus' (schematism). Many scholars at that time believed that Mark, because it was the earliest gospel, had also the greatest historical value. Schmidt agrees that Mark's gospel is the earliest, but asserts that Mark's sketch of the story of Jesus is just as schematic as that of the fourth gospel – i.e. it is, like the Johannine sketch, an attempt to impose on the facts an artificial pattern of the evangelist's creation.[3] Schmidt's analysis of Mark's schematism yields a number of criteria for deciding which parts of the material are Markan and which are taken from tradition.

a) The Criterion of Relevance

Schmidt divides Mark's gospel into sections, each with a dominant theme. He believes that if a story is relevant to the theme of the section in which it occurs, Mark must have placed it at this point for topical reasons; if a story is not relevant to the theme of the section, it must have been already linked in the tradition to a story that was relevant, and Mark must have preserved this linkage despite the inconsistency of the intruding element with his overall design.

The principle is clear – if relevant, Markan; if irrelevant, traditional. Let us look at some examples of the way in which this principle is applied.

We begin with Mark 4. What is the connection between the boat in which Jesus sat to teach (v.1) and the boat in which he crossed the lake (vv.35f.)? It could be that the two pericopes were already linked together in the tradition; or it could be that Mark has brought together two separate pericopes referring to a boat because of the similarity in subject matter. How are we to decide between these two possibilities?

The first essential, Schmidt argues, is to realize that the two pericopes concerned were originally self-contained pericopes and therefore, irrespective of whether they were first connected by Mark or by pre-Markan tradition, this connection is secondary and can be historical only by chance. Having established this as his presupposition, Schmidt then proceeds to decide between the two possibilities by applying the criterion of relevance:

> It is more important to ask the question: with what aim in mind has the evangelist placed the separate stories together? Only if we cannot answer this question does the question as to whether the evangelist may be following an outline that combines the separate stories become significant. We have been able earlier in the book to give a good illustration of the meaning of this two-sided approach in our discussion of 1:21–39 and 2:1–3:6. In the former complex the evangelist had no plan, there was merely a chronological juxtaposition; in the latter complex, on the other hand, the evangelist had a clear plan, and his chronology is therefore doubtful, improbable, impossible.[4]

This principle is then applied to the two boat-references. The section of the gospel in which these verses occur according to Schmidt's plan (3:7–6:13) has as its theme the propaganda activity of Jesus among the people and their rejection of him. The storm story has no obvious relevance to this theme, and this makes it probable that Mark has taken over the link between the two boat-stories from the tradition.[5]

Schmidt passes a similar judgment with regard to the healing of the epileptic boy (Mark 9:14–29). Mark records this story immediately after the descent of Jesus and his three disciples from the mount of transfiguration. Schmidt can see no reason why Mark should have placed the story at this point, since it has nothing to do with the main theme of this section of the gospel. Therefore he concludes that Mark's placement of this story is controlled by the tradition.[6]

In other cases, however, the relevance of a story to Mark's theme indicates a Markan placement. For example, the story of Jesus' rejection at Nazareth (6:1–6) forms the climax of the section 3:7–6:13, whose theme is the hardness of heart and rejection of Jesus by the people. Since Schmidt presupposes that this motif (like all Mark's motifs) was imposed by Mark on his material rather then drawn from the material, the conclusion is clear. 'This fact,' he declares, 'deprives our pericope of any chronological setting.'[7] In other words, whatever is relevant to Mark's theme must *ipso facto* be unhistorical.

The same principle applies to topographical statements such as Mark 10:1: 'And Jesus departed from there and came to the territory of Judaea and Transjordan.' This section of the gospel is a bridge between the Galilee and Jerusalem phases of Jesus' ministry. The passion prophecies have prepared the way for this transition psychologically; physically Mark provides geographical statements which bring us ever closer to Jerusalem. Because of the relevance of this verse to Mark's theme, and because of the generalized nature of the localities mentioned, Schmidt concludes that these words are a Markan editorial addition and that there is therefore no point in asking questions such as 'where exactly did Jesus depart from?'[8]

Passages such as the four just quoted make clear the logical basis of Schmidt's criterion of relevance. This criterion only makes sense if we assume that Mark's plan is total invention – that he had no knowledge at all of the actual sequence of events. Once we allow the possibility that Mark's plan could be based, even to a small degree, on knowledge of the actual sequence of events, then the criterion falls to the ground. For the possibility must then remain in each case that the historical sequence of events could have helped to create Mark's plan rather than the plan dictating the reported sequence of events.

b)   The Criterion of Accidental Transmission

According to this criterion, any detail that the evangelist records by accident is likely to come from early tradition. The clearest statement of this principle occurs in Schmidt's discussion of the Markan complex 6:14–8:26. In this section he regards Mark as on the whole a compiler of unconnected stories: the geographical details in the various stories are in Mark's eyes only a framework, which he has put together without literary art and without concern for the geographical muddle thereby created. But this very fact, that the details have been preserved by chance, makes them especially valuable to the historian. Whereas Luke's location of Jesus' opening sermon in Nazareth (Luke 4:16) is historically worthless, because it serves Luke's purpose for Jesus to begin his ministry in home territory, the mention of place-names such as Bethsaida, Dalmanutha and Magedan serves no special purpose and is therefore historically valuable. 'The evangelist cannot have invented a place-name such as Dalmanutha; but he did not need any special tradition to refer to Galilee.'[9]

Further examples of such 'chance' preservation of details are:

– The reference to the Herodians in Mark 3:6. This does not conform to the normal pattern by which Jesus' enemies are the scribes and Pharisees. Jesus' opposition to the Pharisees was relevant to the situation of the early church, whereas the Herodians disappeared from view. The little information about them in the gospels has been preserved 'so to speak by chance' and is therefore historically valuable.[10]

– The reference to Caesarea Philippi (Mark 8:27), which is unique in Mark, is not required by Mark's itinerary and is not 'schematic' and therefore in Schmidt's judgment belongs to the tradition. Since it has no didactic or symbolic significance, it was not invented by the tradition but is historical fact.[11]

– Schmidt regards Mark's account of the events preceding the passion (10:46–13:37) as a mixture of stories derived from various times and places. However it does contain, in his opinion, some valuable historical information, suggesting in particular that Jesus had visited Jerusalem on previous occasions. This information is to be found in details that Mark has reproduced without any purpose in view, which break through the set pattern he has imposed. For example, the story of blind Bartimaeus (10:46–52) presupposes that the blind man already knew about Jesus; and this suggests that Jesus had worked earlier in the locality.[12]

It is understandable that a critic who regards most of Mark's statements of time and place as historically worthless should wish to distil at least a few statements of historical value. However, the criterion of accidental transmission creates its own problems. It depends on the assumption that we know all the motives that influenced the evangelist, and can therefore decide which references are motiveless. But Schmidt himself admits that we know only a few of Mark's motives.[13] How, then, can we be sure that Bethsaida or Caesarea Philippi or even Dalmanutha did not have a special significance for Mark? There are few if any geographical details in which a modern critic with a good imagination cannot find some hidden significance which would require their rejection as historically worthless on Schmidt's criteria.[14]

My purpose in querying this argument is not to suggest that the references in Mark to Bethsaida, Dalmanutha and Magedan are historically doubtful. I believe that these references are historically accurate, as are also many other Markan references to locations he believes to be significant. My quarrel is with the implication inherent in Schmidt's argument that irrelevance is the *sine qua non* of authenticity – that the only details in Mark's account that are likely to be correct are those to which he attached no significance. To show the absurdity of such a criterion let us imagine a modern parallel.

Let us suppose that a modern historian, Mr. Mark Peterson, writes a book about Sir Winston Churchill's leadership in the Second World War. He believes Churchill was a great leader and records a number of stories that support that belief. But being an honest historian he also records incidents in which Churchill made mistakes. His book is then reviewed by Mr. Charles Ludovic Smith. Smith correctly notes that the book is inspired by the belief that Churchill was a great leader, and argues that all the stories in the book that support that contention should be regarded as tendentious and historically dubious. But there are also stories in the book which describe Churchill's mistakes. These stories, Smith asserts, have crept into the book by chance, without Mr. Peterson (of whose intelligence Smith has a low opinion) realizing their full implications. They are therefore historically reliable, and prove that Churchill was in fact a poor leader.

A little later another book is published. The author of this second book belongs to the debunking school of criticism, and sets out to prove that Churchill was a poor leader. But being an honest historian he records, not only accounts of Churchill's mistakes, but also some accounts of his successes. This book also is reviewed by Mr. Smith. He correctly notes that the book is inspired by the belief that Churchill was a poor leader, and argues that all the stories in the book that support that contention should be regarded as tendentious and historically dubious. But there are also stories in the book that describe Churchill's successes. These stories, Smith asserts, have crept into the book by chance, without the author realizing their full implications. They are therefore historically reliable, and prove that Churchill must have been a great leader after all. In all this Mr. Smith displays a laudable consistency, sticking to his principle that only those facts can be historically reliable which are contrary to the beliefs of the author recording them.

c) The Criterion of Schematic Numbers

A prominent element in Mark's 'Schematismus', according to Schmidt, is his use of schematic numbers. For instance, Mark 3:7–12 describes how people came to Jesus from a wide area. Schmidt points out that seven geographical areas are named. Since seven is a schematic number, this suggests that Mark could have conjured up his list of areas without the help of any special tradition.[15]

Similarly, according to Mark 9:2 the transfiguration of Jesus took place 'after six days'. In Schmidt's opinion the number six is not to be regarded automatically as schematic, like the numbers three and seven, though he does regard as schematic the biblical references to six brothers (Acts 11:12), six jars (John 2:6), six wings (Rev.4:8) and the composite number 606 (Rev.13:18). He discusses the possibility that Mark's six days and the eight days in Luke's transfiguration account may be different ways of saying 'a week later' with exclusive and inclusive reckoning, and also a possible echo of Exodus 24, in which God calls Moses from the cloud on the seventh day after six days of waiting. His conclusion is that some kind of symbolism may or may not be present.[16]

The account of the choosing of the twelve, on the other hand, is described as 'very schematic' with its catalogue of 12 names.[17] Equally suspect is the account of Jesus commissioning the twelve apostles to go on a preaching and healing mission[18], and also Luke's account of the mission of the 70(72). In Schmidt's opinion Luke was right to believe that Jesus commissioned a wider group of disciples, but was 'schematic' in defining the number as 70. Matthew and Mark betray '*Schematismus*' in limiting Jesus' commission to the twelve. But Luke is also guilty of schematism because 70 is another schematic number – and so is 72, if we adopt the alternative reading.[19]

The criterion of schematic numbers is questionable on several grounds. In the first place, how can Schmidt say that the numbers three and seven are automatically (*ohne weiteres*) to be regarded as

schematic? Let us suppose that one of the evangelists reports that a
man has three children. Is it not conceivable that he actually did have
three children? And if he really did have three children, how could the
evangelist report this fact without having his testimony rejected by a
schema-hunting modern critic? The number three is significant in the
twentieth century also. In the game of cricket a bowler who dismisses
three opposing players with successive deliveries is credited with a 'hat
trick', and this threefold achievement is given a significance far
beyond its effect on that particular game. Does this mean that if I read
a report of a hat trick in a newspaper I should automatically dismiss
the report as fictitious because of its schematic nature? If such a
procedure is wrong for a newspaper reader, why is it right for a New
Testament scholar?

The case of the twelve apostles is even more strange, in that
Schmidt accepts that Jesus could have deliberately chosen twelve
apostles to match the number of the twelve tribes.[20] If the choice of
this number does in fact go back to Jesus himself, why should the
evangelists be accused of schematism for attributing to the twelve
disciples twelve names?

Again, how can anyone tell whether Mark deliberately chose seven
geographical areas to portray the spread of Jesus' influence, or
whether the number happened to total seven without his being aware
of it? And even if he did deliberately select seven areas, why should
he not have made his selection from information provided by a source,
whether oral or written?

The attempt to find schematic meanings in numbers makes sense
in the case of an avowedly symbolic book such as the Apocalypse. In
the case of what purport to be historical books, such as the gospels,
the search for schematic relies too much on the critic's presuppositions and too little on concrete evidence. The use of supposedly
schematic numbers as a criterion for lack of historicity has no place
in scientific scholarship.

ii)   Design in Luke

According to Schmidt, Luke's aim is to periodize and psychologize.
In his preface Luke states it as his aim to describe events in their proper
order. But, in Schmidt's opinion, when Luke's alterations to Mark are
checked, they do not suggest that he is introducing new topographical
or chronological facts drawn from a special tradition, but rather that,

in order to make the story hold together better, he alters Mark for reasons of psychology and logic. Luke, he concludes, was not a great scholar and researcher but a clever author. Not having any new sources he simply regrouped and reorganized the material to hand.[21]

Schmidt claims that this evaluation of Luke is borne out by the comments made in the course of the book. As we now turn to some of these comments, we shall be asking the question: is Schmidt's oft-repeated assertion that Luke did not research facts but invented them based on concrete evidence, or on the principle that if you say something often enough, people are going to believe it?

a) In his account of the healing of the paralysed man Mark refers to 'some scribes who were sitting there' (2:6); but Luke in the parallel passage states that there were sitting there 'Pharisees and teachers of the law who had come from every village in Galilee and Judaea and Jerusalem.' (5:17). This statement, Schmidt declares, is 'naturally' (natürlich) not based on a special Lukan tradition. The word 'naturally' is presumably an appeal to dogma – in every such case it is to be assumed that Luke had no source but Mark.[22]

b) Luke alone states that, before selecting the twelve, Jesus spent the night in prayer (6:12). Schmidt considers this to be an addition by the evangelist, who was able in this way to set an originally timeless story into a chronological framework. It is also a psychological style of presentation, which is characteristic of Luke.[23]

c) Luke is the only evangelist to record that the daughter of Jairus was his only daughter. It is unnecessary, Schmidt declares, to assume that Luke gathered this from a special tradition. He could easily have distilled it from the story as a whole, which spoke only of father, mother and acquaintances.[24]

d) In Schmidt's opinion, Luke has on various occasions provided a detailed background without the support of any tradition. He instances 10:1, where the sending out of the seventy on mission is given a graphic introduction, and 11:39ff., where a series of denunciations of scribes and Pharisees (with many parallels in Matthew 23) is prefaced by an account of a Pharisee who invited Jesus for a meal and noticed that he did not carry out the ritual washing before the meal. The only evidence adduced for ascribing these details to Luke's power of invention is the fact that they are written in a typically Lukan style. But style can be used as an indication of the presence or absence of sources only if we assume that Luke was not an author but a copyist, who invariably reproduced the exact language of his sources as well as their factual content.[25]

e)　In recording the triumphal entry Luke is the only evangelist to name a precise geographical location. According to Luke 19:37 it was near to the descent of the Mount of Olives that the crowd began to shout 'Blessed is the king who comes in the name of the Lord!' Earlier scholars such as B. Weiss and Spitta had seen in this statement the influence of a special Lukan source with precise knowledge of the topography of Jerusalem. But Schmidt argues that too much has been made of this passage, which 'reveals without question its character as an explanatory comment by Luke, who did not need for this purpose any special geographical knowledge.' The use of the phrase 'without question' (*ohne weiteres*) is characteristic of Schmidt's approach. It is true that Luke *could* have arrived at this statement by clever deduction from his Markan source without having any personal knowledge of Jerusalem or access to any other source. But Schmidt assumes without question that this is what *did* happen.[26]

The conversion of possibilities into certainties is the basis of Schmidt's argument in all the passages we have considered. The argument runs as follows: Luke has added such-and-such to Mark's narrative; he did not need to have special sources of information but could have invented this extra material out of his own head; therefore this is what in fact he did. The final point is not always stated but is always implied, and is logically required by Schmidt's assertion that at no point (*nirgends*) did Luke engage in careful research.[27] Allegations of this sort are impossible to prove or disprove. Since we have no means of checking most of the statements peculiar to Luke, our assessment of them will depend on our presuppositions. Those who have a high opinion of Luke as a historian will assume that he had other sources; those like Schmidt who have a low opinion of Luke as a historian will assume that he invented the facts in the interests of psychology and logic.

　　At the same time there is something almost pathological about Schmidt's refusal to accept the possibility of any separate tradition that Luke could draw on. He accepts that Luke had other sources for his travel narrative. It is only when there is a parallel in Mark that Luke has no other source. This presupposes that Luke's other sources never overlapped with Mark, or that if they did Luke steadfastly refused to consider any other source if Mark lay to hand. One wonders how Schmidt can be so sure that this was the case.

In fact Schmidt is not totally consistent. Luke writes that Mary travelled to 'a town in Judah' to visit Elizabeth (1:39). Schmidt comments that Luke would have fixed the name of the place more precisely if the tradition had provided more definite information, but that it was not his habit to pluck supplementary facts out of the air. This judgment seems strange after Schmidt has been treating Luke's supplementary facts as plucked out of the air throughout the book.[28]

Another passage that seems to go against the trend is his comment on Luke 8:1–3. Luke names a group of women who travelled with Jesus and the twelve giving practical help: Mary Magdalene, Joanna the wife of Chuza, Susanna and 'many others'. In Mark 15:40f. there is a similar list of women who travelled to Jerusalem with Jesus and watched the crucifixion: Mary Magdalene, Mary the mother of James and Joses, Salome and 'many others'. Since the named women are so different in the two passages, and both Mark and Luke state that the names given are only a selection from a wider group, it has often been assumed that Mark and Luke were following different sources. Schmidt, however, argues that Luke is following Mark here, but has transferred the Markan statement to an earlier point in the narrative because of his desire to periodize. At the same time he admits that the details of the Lukan passage are not drawn from Mark and comments that we cannot tell whether Luke is following oral or written tradition. So there is at least one passage in Luke which Schmidt believes to be based on Mark but also to draw on other tradition. One wonders why this possibility has not been recognized in many other passages.[29]

In his discussion of the Lukan Travel Narrative (9:51–19:27) Schmidt attempts to distinguish the statements of time and place Luke has composed himself from those he has received from his sources. One of his main criteria is the criterion of relevance. Those introductory statements that emphasize that Jesus is travelling and drawing near to Jerusalem are invented by Luke, since they bring out the main theme of the section.[30] But if Schmidt cannot think of any reason for Luke to have invented an introductory statement he attributes it to tradition. For example, the teaching elements in this section are introduced in a variety of ways, such as καὶ εἶπεν πρὸ ς αὐτούς (and he said to them) (11:5), κἀγὼ ὑμῖν λέγω (and I say to you) (11:9), ἔλεγεν οὖν (so he said) (13:18). Schmidt can see no reason for Luke to vary the introductory phrases in this manner, so inclines to the view that he is following tradition.[31] Similarly, he can see no reason for Luke to locate Zacchaeus in Jericho unless he received this location from the tradition.[32] Again, the story of the crippled woman (13:10–17) does not fit well into its Lukan context, so we may assume that it was already linked in Luke's source to the material preceding or following it.[33] Where Schmidt can see no reason for Luke to locate material at a particular point and no reason for the tradition to do so either, he falls back on the theory of author fatigue. There is no obvious reason for the sayings in 16:16–18 to be placed where they are, so Schmidt comments that at various places Luke clearly got tired and located sayings as best he could without any clear sequence of thought.[34]

The criterion of relevance is no sounder when applied to Luke than we have seen it to be when applied to Mark. Firstly, it rests on the assumption that a modern critic can so read the mind of an ancient author as to understand fully the sum total of that author's motivation. For example, Schmidt cannot see any reason for Luke to vary his introductory formulae, and assumes from this that Luke in fact did not have any such reason. But Luke was a stylist, and for a stylist variety is a reason in itself. Schmidt's comment reveals the deficiency of his imagination, rather than Luke's limitations.

Secondly, the tendentious motives that Schmidt reads into Luke's mind may not always have been there. Luke records some sayings of Jesus about his being perfected on the third day and journeying on the third day (13:32f.). Schmidt asserts that Luke has altered the sense of an early Christian confession, and when he mentions the third day is clearly thinking of the fact that Jesus is three days' journey away from Jerusalem.[35] Attempts such as this to read Luke's mind do not always carry conviction and suggest that Schmidt's confidence in his own psychological judgment may not always be justified.

Thirdly, even if Luke was highly motivated to make a particular statement, that statement could still be based on tradition. Schmidt admits this in the case of the Samaritan village that refused to receive Jesus (Luke 9: 51–56). He believes this story to be very relevant to the situation of Samaritan Christians and the mission politics of Luke's day. It is also the linchpin on which the whole travel narrative depends. Nevertheless, Schmidt thinks it inconceivable that Luke could have invented the story. 'One must admit,' he writes, 'that the story has colour and creates an impression of historicity.' So he argues that Luke took a story about Jesus' activity in Samaria that was available in his sources and used it as a peg upon which to hang the whole Travel Narrative.[36] But if this story which fits Luke's purpose so well was already in his source and was already set in its correct geographical location, why should this not be true of other stories and geographical locations? What becomes of the criterion that, if a statement suits Luke's purpose, he must have invented it?

iii) Conclusion

The *argument from design* is a product of the nineteenth-century opposition between facts and interpretation – the idea that one can separate pure facts from biased interpretation. According to E.H. Carr the challenge to what he calls 'the doctrine of the primacy and autonomy of facts in history' began in Germany in the late nineteenth century with philosophers such as Dilthey, but became influential only after the First World War.[37] Today many would agree with Carr's assertion that 'history means interpretation'.[38] This is true of the first-century evangelist who understood the life of Jesus in the light of his religious experience within the early church, and is equally true of the twentieth-century scholar who understands the life of Jesus in the light of current trends in gospel scholarship. Which of these evaluations of the historical data is nearer the truth is a matter of opinion, but the fact that both first-century evangelists and twentieth-century scholars start from a theological base does not in itself prove anything about the accuracy of the statements they make. In the words of Martin Hengel:

> The fatal error in the interpretation of the Gospels in general and of Mark in particular has been that scholars have thought that they had to decide between preaching and historical narration, that there could only be an either-or. In reality the 'theological' contribution of the evangelist lies in the fact that he combines both these things inseparably: he preaches by narrating; he writes history and in doing so proclaims. . . . At this point he has the model of Old Testament historiography before him, where this unity of narration and proclamation is often visible.[39]

Mark's account of the life of the son of David is, like the account of the life of David in 1 and 2 Samuel, at the same time *both* a historical *and* a prophetic work.

Notes

1 For a more general consideration of the *argument from design* in New Testament study, see Hall, *Seven Pillories* 30–35.

2   Schmidt, *Rahmen* 316.
3   Ibid. 17.
4   Ibid. 137f.
5   Ibid. 138.
6   Ibid. 227.
7   Ibid. 153.
8   Ibid. 238f.
9   Ibid. 209f., 219.
10   Ibid. 100f.
11   Ibid. 216.
12   Ibid. 301–3.
13   Ibid. 180: 'Mark compiled his stories from internal and external motives. We do
     not know these motives and can demonstrate only a small part of them. Purely
     literary considerations help us in this task.'
14   According to Telford, *Interpretation* 34: 'the theological nature of Marcan
     geography is being increasingly asserted.' He quotes not only W. Marxsen's
     pioneering argument for the theological nature of Mark's references to Galilee,
     but also more recent works on the significance for Gentile-Jew relationships of
     the visit to Tyre and Sidon or the crossings of the lake, and various structuralist
     treatments of Marcan geography (59 n.20).
15   Schmidt, *Rahmen* 106.
16   Ibid. 223.
17   Ibid. 110.
18   Ibid. 164.
19   Ibid. 169: 'Mark and Matthew, by limiting the mission to the twelve, provide a
     suprahistorical style of presentation, an unhistorical schematism, which re-
     quired to be criticized. Luke offers this criticism, even though through lack of
     genuine historical material he also does not escape from schematism – for 70 is
     also a schematic number.' Schmidt has shown earlier (167) that 72 is also a holy
     number in Jewish tradition.
20   Schmidt, *Rahmen* 168.
21   Ibid. 316.
22   Ibid. 81.
23   Ibid. 112.
24   Ibid. 148.
25   Ibid. 259.
26   Ibid. 298 n.1.
27   Ibid. 316: 'In his prologue the author purports to be providing something special
     particularly in the area of accuracy and the sequence of events. But we have been
     able to check how time after time he does not go beyond Mark, for example, by
     introducing new chronological or topographical data into the story of Jesus on
     the basis of a separate tradition; rather, in his concern to make the narrative hold
     together better, he alters Mark's outline for reasons of psychology and logic. For
     this he did not need at any point to undertake research in depth; all he needed
     was a kind of trained literary taste.'
28   Ibid. 311.
29   Ibid. 129.
30   Ibid. 260.
31   Ibid. 257f.

32   Ibid. 264f.
33   Ibid. 271.
34   Ibid. 271.
35   Ibid. 266.
36   Ibid. 268f.
37   Edward Hallett Carr, *What is History?* (Penguin, Harmondsworth 1964) 20f.
38   Ibid. 23.
39   Martin Hengel, *Studies in the Gospel of Mark* tr. John Bowden (SCM, London 1985) 41.

3

The Argument From Contradiction

One of Schmidt's favourite tactics is to point out supposed logical inconsistencies in Mark's narrative. As well as the full contradiction (*Widerspruch*), there is also the difficulty (*Schwierigkeit*), the inconsistency (*Unausgeglichenheit*), awkwardness (*Inkonzinnität*), clumsiness (*Ungeschicklichkeit*) and discrepancy (*Unstimmigkeit*). The technique for discovering all these faults is the same. Mark's words are interpreted absolutely literally and then declared to be inconsistent with each other. Any attempt to reconstruct the original historical situation by the use of imagination is rejected – for one thing, such attempts mean reading into the text something that is not expressly there; for another thing, such attempts involve 'harmonization' and are therefore suspect on principle; but most importantly of all, such attempts do not recognize the nature of Mark's editorial technique and the low level of Mark's intelligence.

Inevitably this chapter will involve consideration of a large number of small details. But it is important to do this. Schmidt's aim in pointing out all these alleged faults is to portray Mark as a clumsy collector of miscellaneous stories which he has placed side by side without realizing, or bothering about, the inconsistencies in the narrative. The only way to evaluate this portrait of Mark is to examine these 'inconsistencies' one by one and ask the question whether Schmidt's critical techniques prove his case or not.

1. Mark 1:9 states that Jesus came from Nazareth and was baptized by John in the Jordan. Schmidt observes that the words 'in the Jordan' are unnecessary, since it is clear from the preceding verses that any baptism by John would inevitably be in the Jordan. He confesses that this observation might seem to many people to be of no importance, but in his case it leads him to the conclusion

that verses 9–11 were originally an independent pericope, which Mark has artlessly (*ohne Kunst*) attached to verses 4–8.[1]

This judgment raises an important matter of principle. There have been many critics over the years who have criticized Mark on aesthetic grounds, implying that, had they written the gospel themselves, they could have made a better job of it. The question is, are such subjective judgments admissible as evidence for dividing Mark up among separate sources? The particular issue here is repetition. Repetition is often unnecessary from a logical point of view but artistically valuable. For example, the passion predictions in 9:31 and 10:33f. are essentially repetitions of the passion prediction in 8:31; but this does not make them artless, nor does it indicate separate sources. Schmidt's judgment with regard to the repetition of Jordan seems to me to be evidence, not for the process by which Mark's gospel was composed, but for the limitations of logic in literary criticism.

It is interesting to compare Schmidt's attitude with that of E.V. Rieu, the translator of Homer. In the preface to his translation of the Odyssey Rieu discusses Homer's use of recurring epithets:

> Then there are a number of curious cases in which, unless we credit him with self-conscious art, Homer must be regarded as having used a stereotyped expression in a meaningless way, or as having 'nodded' – which would amount to the same thing for such a stylist. I take it as an axiom that Homer never nods, and I suggest that where (in xxiv.57) he gives the Achaeans their usual epithet of 'great-hearted', though they are behaving like cowards, he does so in order to produce an exactly opposite effect – and succeeds. . . . Dogs are styled 'noisy', and rightly so in xiv.29, when they bark at a stranger, but somewhat surprisingly also in xvi.4, where they are greeting a friend and are expressly stated not to have barked. Here the meaning, and the translation 'usually so obstreperous', are easily arrived at.[2]

There are, of course, considerable differences between Homer and Mark, and the use of recurrent epithets is a far more prominent feature of Homer's style than of Mark's. I am not suggesting that Rieu's remarks about Homer can be applied to Mark as they stand. What is interesting is the contrast in attitude between Rieu and Schmidt. Rieu's discussion is based on a deep respect for Homer, even in an area where Homer's technique is quite different from that of a twentieth-century poet, and where Homer's use of that technique has been called into question by sceptical scholars. Schmidt's discussion, on the other hand, is based on a deep contempt for Mark, which leads him to condemn any deviation from his logical conception of how authors should write.

2.　The issue of repetition recurs in Schmidt's comment on the account of Judas's betrayal in Mark 14. Mark describes how 'Judas Iscariot, one of the twelve' arranged with the high priests to betray Jesus (vv.10f.). Later in the same chapter we read that 'Judas, one of the twelve' came with a crowd of armed men to Gethsemane (v.43). Schmidt objects that in verse 43 Judas is referred to as one of the twelve for the second time as though we had never heard of him before. Moreover, he alleges that the description of Judas's interview with the high priests is not as graphic as it ought to be and is not anchored in a clear situation. These deficiencies suggest to him that this interview is a Markan creation, developed out of the Gethsemane story which he received from the tradition.[3]

Let us look at some of these points in detail. Schmidt's main objection is that the words 'one of the twelve' are repeated when they are not logically necessary. In point of fact, he could have argued that the reference to Judas as one of the twelve in verse 10 is also superfluous, since the fact that Judas was one of the twelve was already known to Mark's readers from 3:19. Thinking about this argument, I began to wonder how Schmidt would have expounded the Book of Psalms. It would be fascinating to read a commentary on Psalms based on the principle that any repetition that is not logically necessary betrays a plurality of sources.

The phrase 'one of the twelve' runs like a refrain through chapter 14, occurring not only in the two verses mentioned by Schmidt but also in verse 20, where Jesus says that one of the twelve will betray him. This threefold repetition is more likely to reflect the deep shock inflicted by Judas's betrayal on the early disciples than to indicate Mark's literary shortcomings.

Schmidt also objects that Mark's account is not graphic enough and is not anchored in a clear situation. Subjective judgments of this sort appear regularly throughout the book. Again and again we are told of a lack of vividness (*Anschaulichkeit*) in Mark's narrative, or of a lack of proper colour (*rechte Farbe*), and these deficiencies are attributed to Mark's clumsy handiwork. On the other hand, if Mark had given details of exactly where and when Judas interviewed the high priests, Schmidt would probably have regarded these details as added by Mark to give verisimilitude to his story, and if Mark had commented on Judas's state of mind and motivation, Schmidt would probably have dismissed these comments as 'psychologizing' – his favourite charge against Luke whenever Luke makes comments of this kind.[4] It is difficult to think of any way in which the evangelists could have expressed themselves without being exposed to one or another of these charges.

3. In Mark 1:38 Jesus says: 'Let us go to the nearby villages so that I can preach there.' Mark then describes how Jesus travelled through Galilee, preaching and casting out demons. The reference to casting out demons is in Schmidt's opinion an example of awkwardness (*Inkonzinnität*), because in the previous verse Jesus said simply that he was going to preach.

Schmidt refuses to follow earlier scholars in removing the reference to demons as an interpolation; rather, he sees it as an example of Mark's clumsy workmanship – Mark wished to give a broad picture of the ministry of Jesus, but failed to assimilate his picture to the words he had just taken over from the tradition.[5]

This is a prime example of Schmidt's literalism. Because the saying of Jesus in verse 38 does not expressly mention exorcism, Schmidt takes it to mean that Jesus intended to preach and do nothing else: if sick people came to him, he would presumably refuse to help them, because his mission was solely to preach. I find it incredible that Jesus could have meant this, or that early church tradition could have thought that Jesus meant this, or that Mark could have thought that Jesus meant this. If a modern minister tells me that he or she has been invited to preach in a certain place, I do not assume from this statement that the minister concerned will do nothing but preach – will refuse to lead public worship, or to pray for the sick if requested, or to counsel people in need. This sort of pedantic literalism seems to betray a total misunderstanding of the character of Jesus.

4. At the end of chapter 1 Mark recounts how Jesus healed a man of leprosy, and how the man started to tell everyone what had happened. As a result, 'Jesus could no longer go openly into town, but stayed outside in lonely places, and people came to him from all directions.' (v.45).

In this verse Schmidt finds an 'inner contradiction' (*innere Widerspruch*). We expect the words 'he could no longer go openly into town' to continue 'but he could only enter secretly'; but instead of this we are told that Jesus did not enter a town at all but stayed in lonely places. This inner contradiction within verse 45 seems to Schmidt to be more important than the often alleged contradiction between verse 45 and the following verse (2:1), which refers to Jesus entering Capernaum.

Various scholars before Schmidt had rejected the whole of verse 45 as a Markan addition. Schmidt prefers to see most of verse 45 as belonging to the tradition, to which Mark has added the one word 'openly' (φανερῶς). Mark's purpose in adding this word was to make verse 45 fit in with the following verse (2:1) which implied a secret entry into Capernaum. But by adding the word, Schmidt argues, Mark has spoilt the balance of verse 45, which reads much better without it.[6]

This whole discussion exemplifies the literalism we have already noted. Mark's statements in verse 45 are not absolutes but generalizations. The publicity meant that Jesus could not enter a town publicly. From time to time he would enter one secretly (as in 2:1), but most of the time he kept to lonely places. Mark's wording is abbreviated but perfectly understandable. In making his objection Schmidt reveals what he means by a contradiction. The two statements 'he could not enter a town openly' and 'he stayed in lonely places' are not contradictory in any formal sense. The contradiction, as Schmidt makes clear, is between what Mark wrote and what a pedantic scholar would expect him to have written. Mark has not so much failed to be understandable as failed to be strictly logical.

5.   In the story of the call of Levi and the meal at his house (Mark 2:13–17) Schmidt finds an inner contradiction between verses 14 and 15. In verse 14 Jesus calls Levi to be a disciple, whereas verse 15, in Schmidt's opinion, presupposes that the circle of disciples is already complete.[7] Presumably he understands the words 'Jesus and his disciples' in verse 15 to be equivalent to 'Jesus and the twelve'. But this is not the case. The phrase 'his disciples' means 'those disciples who were present at the time' and can refer to a number either larger or smaller than the twelve, just as 'the Pharisees' in 2:24 does not mean 'all the Pharisees in Judaea' but 'those Pharisees who were present on this occasion'. Later in the book, when discussing the triumphal entry, Schmidt observes how in Matthew and Mark Jesus is acclaimed by the general public, but in Luke by 'the multitude of the disciples' (τὸ πλῆθος τῶν μαθητῶν). He comments that the difference between the two versions is not great, because Luke does not restrict the word 'disciple' to the twelve but is thinking of a large number of adherents.[8] The same could be said of Mark. Mark 3:13f. implies that the twelve were selected out of a wider group of disciples,

and Mark 4:10 refers to 'those around Jesus including the twelve'. The idea that there could not have been any group identifiable as disciples of Jesus before the official selection of the twelve is an idea Schmidt has read into the text, not drawn from it.

6. The healing of the man with the withered hand is related in Matthew, Mark and Luke. Matthew's account begins with the words: 'and Jesus departed from there and entered their synagogue' (καὶ μεταβὰς ἐκεῖθεν ἦλθεν εἰς τὴν συναγωγὴν αὐτῶν) (12:9). According to Schmidt these words mean that the healing took place on the same sabbath as the plucking of the ears of corn described in the previous story (12:1–8). Therefore Matthew's account is contradicted by Luke's statement (6:6) that this healing took place on another sabbath.[9]

The point at issue is: what does Matthew mean by the words 'he departed from there' (μεταβὰς ἐκεῖθεν)? Does he mean, as Schmidt assumes, that Jesus moved directly, the same day, from the previous venue to the synagogue?

The word μεταβαίνω (depart) occurs five times in Matthew. In 8:34 the Gadarenes ask Jesus to depart from their territory; in 11:1 Jesus departs from one place in order to teach and preach in surrounding towns; in 15:29 Jesus moves from the region of Tyre and Sidon to the Sea of Galilee; in 17:20 Jesus says that those who have faith can order a mountain to move from its place to somewhere else. Thus the other four occurrences of this verb in Matthew refer to removal from one geographical area to another. There are no grounds for Schmidt's assumption that in the fifth case Matthew means merely a sabbath-day's journey to the nearest synagogue.

7. Commenting on Matthew's Sermon on the Mount and Luke's Sermon on the Plain, Schmidt detects a discrepancy (*Unstimmigkeit*) in both cases. The sermons are addressed to the disciples, but the crowd is listening. In the case of Luke he declares that 'this discrepancy cannot be explained away.' His explanation for the discrepancy is that the content of the sermons is taken from Q, in which the teaching is addressed only to the disciples, whereas the evangelists pictured the sermons in their own minds as being delivered to a large crowd.[10]

This is a good example of how to convert molehills into mountains. Schmidt concedes that in Q (as in Luke 6:20) the term 'disciples' is not limited to the twelve, but includes a great number of adherents. He also refers to Luke 20:45, where Jesus speaks to the disciples in the hearing of the whole people, and regards this as another example of Luke's imaginative expansion of an audience that was limited to disciples only in his source. But in fact the situation Luke envisages is perfectly clear. A large crowd gathers round Jesus, including hundreds of people who would identify themselves as his followers and hundreds of others who are uncommitted or have come out of curiosity. Whichever group he was addressing, Jesus would have to lift up his voice with strength in order to be heard, and everybody would hear what was being said. In such a situation any distinction between words addressed to committed disciples and words addressed to the uncommitted would depend on the nature of the words concerned, and it would be possible to gear various parts of the same sermon to various segments of the audience.

Some years ago I attended a rally in a football stadium addressed by Dr. Billy Graham. In response to his appeal for commitment to Christ several hundred people left their seats and walked on to the pitch. Dr. Graham then addressed some words especially to these people, but his words were broadcast over the PA system and were heard by everybody. A similar situation arises at a railway station when travellers waiting for a particular train are given information over the PA system that everyone can hear. When I picture the public preaching of Jesus in my imagination, it is images such as these that come to mind.

Presumably such an understanding of the situation would count in Schmidt's eyes as 'explaining away' (*hinweginterpretieren*) a logical discrepancy. By contrast, his own understanding – that both Matthew and Luke recorded inconsistent descriptions of the same event without realizing what they were doing – counts as legitimate interpretation, reflecting his low opinion of the intelligence of the authors concerned.

8.   Schmidt's treatment of Mark 4:1–34 illustrates the way in which, for him, logical consistency is the key to literary criticism. The chapter begins with Jesus in a boat on the lake and a crowd of listeners on the shore. Jesus begins to teach them in parables and in the course of his teaching tells the parable of the sower. Afterwards his disciples ask him privately about the parables, and he comments on parables in general and then explains the parable of the sower. From verse 21 onwards there follows a series of parables introduced by the words καὶ ἔλεγεν αὐτοῖς (and he said to them) and καὶ ἔλεγεν (and he said). Mark concludes (vv.33f.) with a general comment on Jesus's use of parables.

In the latter part of this section (vv.21–34) all the editorial verbs are in the imperfect tense. The parables Mark records may have been spoken by Jesus on various occasions and repeated in various places, and Mark has collected them here for convenience. This is one of the passages in Mark where Schmidt's theory that Mark was not interested in time or place makes sense, and where Mark's presentation itself supports that theory. The problem is that Schmidt, with his usual concern for logical consistency, tries to impose the same theory on verses 1–20, whose style is quite different – some of the editorial verbs are in the aorist or present tense, and Mark clearly intends to portray a sequence of specific events. Schmidt's theory is that verses 1–9, verses 10–12 and verses 13–20 were originally separate units, which Mark has strung together in the same way as the parables are strung together in verses 21–32. At first sight this seems an odd theory – that the parable of the sower and the interpretation of the parable of the sower circulated independently of each other – but the logic of Schmidt's argument seems to require him to propose it.[11]

As usual, this theory is supported by the detection of a logical inconsistency. The disciples, Schmidt asserts, ask in verse 10 a question about parables in general, whereas in the preceding verses only one parable has been named. This means, we are told, that there is no proper connection between verse 10 and the preceding section, and is an example of Mark's carelessness about context.[12] This seems a very strange criticism. According to Mark 4:2f. Jesus 'taught them many things in parables, and said in the course of his teaching: "Listen: a sower went out to sow . . ." '. Mark could hardly have stated more clearly that the parable of the sower was not spoken on its own but was one parable among many. Whatever questions may be raised about the *content* of verses 10–12, the *context* runs perfectly smoothly.[13]

9.   According to Mark 5:21, after the healing of the Gerasene demoniac Jesus crossed over again to the other side of the lake (καὶ διαπεράσαντος τοῦ Ἰησοῦ πάλιν εἰς τὸ πέραν....). Schmidt comments that other scholars do not find any difficulty in this statement; but that does not prevent him from doing so. His difficulty is that τὸ πέραν (the other side) normally refers to the east bank of the Sea of Galilee (or of the Jordan), whereas the Markan text envisages a crossing to the west bank. The words simply mean 'the other side' and there is no grammatical difficulty in a crossing from east to west or from south to north. Schmidt's difficulty is that the other Synoptic occurrences the phrase in fact refers to the east bank; and the phrase πέραν τοῦ

Ἰορδάνου (the other side of the Jordan) is sometimes used as a geographical term to refer to Peraea, the province east of the Jordan. Therefore, being a lover of consistency, he suggests that in Mark's source the phrase had its usual connotation of a crossing from west to east, and that Mark has taken over the words and placed them in a context where they convey a completely opposite meaning.[14]

One problem with Schmidt's interpretation is that there is a clear case in John's gospel (6:17) where a crossing to 'the other side' ends up on the west bank: καὶ ἐμβάντες εἰς πλοῖον ἤρχοντο πέραν τῆς θαλάσσης εἰς καφαρναούμ (and entering a boat they travelled to the other side of the lake to Capernaum). Schmidt suggests that in this verse πέραν τῆς θαλάσσης should be translated *'from* the other side of the lake'. He cites as a parallel Mark 3:8, where Mark states that the followers of Jesus came 'from Jerusalem and from Idumaea and beyond the Jordan and the vicinity of Tyre and Sidon' (ἀπὸ Ἱεροσολύμων καὶ ἀπὸ τῆς Ἰδουμαίας καὶ πέραν τοῦ Ἰορδάνου καὶ περὶ Τύρον καὶ Σιδῶνα). But this is not a real parallel. In Mark 3:8 the phrases πέραν τοῦ Ἰορδάνου and περὶ Τύρον καὶ Σιδῶνα are both governed by the preposition ἀπὸ – the idea of 'coming from' is entirely derived from that preposition, and there is no ground for the suggestion that πέραν *in itself* means 'from the other side of' or that, in the case of Tyre and Sidon, περὶ *in itself* means 'from the vicinity of'. I do not know of any other scholar who has followed Schmidt in twisting the plain meaning of John's words. His argument reveals the extraordinary lengths to which he is prepared to go in order to find difficulties where none exist.

10. In Mark 5 and Luke 8 the account of the healing of Jairus' daughter comes immediately after the healing of the Gerasene demoniac; but Matthew includes between these two accounts several other stories, such as the healing of the paralysed man, which appear much earlier in Mark and Luke. Upholders of the Markan hypothesis had regarded Mark as giving these events in their correct order and Matthew's sequence of events as inferior. But Schmidt objects to this. He believes that for both Mark and Matthew the order of events is determined purely by theological and pragmatic considerations.

In support of this hypothesis Schmidt ridicules the sequence of events presented by Mark. Jesus preaches to the people (4:1ff.); in the evening or late afternoon he crosses the lake (4:35); after reaching the other side he heals the demoniac (5:1–20), travels back across the lake, is invited to Jairus' house, heals a woman on the way and raises to life Jairus' daughter (5:21–43). All this, Schmidt declares, happened according to Mark on the same day! Since this is clearly absurd, scholars either emend the text or postulate a time interval between 5:20 and 5:21. But in Schmidt's opinion these are attempts to escape from a dilemma (*Verlegenheitsauskünfte*), based on a misunderstanding of Mark's literary technique and on the false view that there is a chronological thread running through his gospel.[15]

Now if Schmidt were correct in claiming that Mark has crowded all these events into one day, his criticism of Mark's stupidity and the scholars' evasiveness would be justified. But Mark's narrative implies no such thing. Mark 5:21f. reads as follows: 'And when Jesus had crossed over again to the other side of the lake, a great crowd gathered round him, and he was by the lakeside, and a ruler of the synagogue named Jairus came. . . .' Mark does not state how much time elapsed between the healing of the demoniac and the return crossing, between the landing and the gathering of the crowd, or between the gathering of the crowd and the appearance of Jairus. Schmidt's theory that all this happened on one day has no support in the text. I can only presume that he is relying on the argument from silence: since Mark does not *mention* a specific time interval, he cannot have believed that there was one.

I often watch TV programmes that present edited highlights of games of football. The games last for an hour and a half. The highlights of each game may last for 20 minutes or less. But the selection of highlights is so skilfully done that I am often not aware of the passage of time, and the programme gives the illusion of a continuous game. In some ways Mark's technique was similar. The ministry of Jesus lasted probably for several years. Mark's selected highlights cover a few pages. To make the best use of the limited space available, Mark has not cluttered his narrative with time statements – that this event took place a day or a week or two months after that event – but has telescoped his highlights into a continuous story-line.

In the case of football programmes the highlights are presented in chronological order. How far Mark has attempted to do the same is a debatable issue; and his use of the 'selected highlights' technique is one factor in the debate. Windisch's suggestion of a lapse of time between the healing of the demoniac and the crossing of the lake, which Schmidt dismisses as an attempt to escape from a dilemma, may in fact indicate that Windisch understood Mark's editorial technique better than Schmidt.[16]

If we call into question Schmidt's assumption that the gospels are chronologically worthless, we are faced with questions such as this: did the healing of the paralysed man take place before the healing of the demoniac (as in Mark) or after (as in Matthew)? Schmidt is surely right to insist that, where the order of events in Mark and Matthew differs, we should not automatically prefer Mark. But in most cases it is not possible to go beyond that and give a firm answer to such questions. Both Matthew and Mark present edited highlights, and in this case one or other of them has transposed the order of events. The significance of this should be noted but not exaggerated. On the one hand, there are a number of instances where the order of events differs between the gospels. On the other hand, both Matthew and Luke follow the Markan order in the majority of cases – indeed, it is this correspondence in order that constitutes for many scholars the main reason for assuming literary dependence between the three gospels. Schmidt is correct to point out that, where the gospels disagree, the order of events in at least one of them must be unchronological. It does not follow from this, as he believes, that all three synoptic gospels are consistently unchronological.

11.   One of the quaint features of the argument from contradiction is the assumption that a particular tradition will always refer to the same person in the same way. If a person is referred to in two different ways in the same context, this is taken to indicate either separate traditions or editorial interpolation. For example, Mark records in 6:7 that Jesus sent out 'the twelve' on mission; but in 6:30 it is 'the apostles' who return. Schmidt's explanation is that Mark is following two separate traditions, which did not originally refer to the same situation.[17] One might think that, since Mark uses the word ἀποστέλλειν to describe the sending out of the missioners, the corresponding noun ἀπόστολος would be an appropriate term to define them. But Schmidt's belief that Mark follows blindly the exact wording of his sources, and that those sources would be bound to refer to the missioners by exactly the same title throughout, prevents him from crediting Mark with such a degree of creativity.

A similar situation arises with the story of Jairus (5:21–43). Mark refers to Jairus first by name (v.22) and then by title as the leader of the synagogue (vv.35,38). This, to quote Schmidt's words, is 'stylistically not totally objection-free', and makes it 'not totally improbable' that the mention of Jairus' name is an interpolation. His preferred solution is to regard Mark simply as a copyist and to locate the problem at an earlier stage in the tradition. The inconsistency in the naming of Jairus suggests to him that the name was added to the pre-Markan tradition at some stage in its development, in the same way as the woman who touched Jesus's garment was given the name Veronica in later legend.[18] Strangely, Schmidt does not seem to notice the fact that Jairus is referred to in a third way in v.40 as 'the father of the child'.

This insistence on uniformity of description may reflect the fact that Schmidt had not read many Russian novels; but he also seems to be unaware of how common such alternations are in the gospel narratives. For instance, Matthew mentions the name Caiaphas in 26:57 but thereafter uses the title 'highpriest'. Similarly Pilate is normally referred to by title as governor. Matthew refers to him by name in 27:2 and thereafter mainly as 'the governor'. In Matthew 27:11–26 we find the title four times and the name Pilate four times. What Schmidt would have made of this had he discussed it I do not know. Would he have suggested that Matthew was interweaving two sources or that all the references to Pilate by name were Matthaean interpolations?

My own impression when reading this kind of criticism is that Schmidt had no 'feel' for literature and literary style. The type of literature he was accustomed to was technical scholarly literature, in which each word had as precise and distinct a meaning as possible; and he insisted on applying the standards of that literature to writings of a completely different kind.

12. In chapter 6 Mark describes how the disciples, after the feeding of the five thousand, set out in a boat to cross to Bethsaida (v.45). After being caught in a storm they eventually land at Gennesaret (v.53). Schmidt finds this difficult (*schwierig*). The common explanation is that they were blown off course by the wind. Any expositor who takes this line, Schmidt declares, must be conscious that he is introducing new ideas into the text (*dass er hier Eintragungen vollzieht*). Presumably it is this that he finds difficult.[19]

I cannot myself see where the difficulty lies. Mark's narrative provides an original destination, a severe storm and a final destination. He presumably credited his readers with the intelligence to see the connection between these events without needing to spell it out in detail. Inevitably the use of intelligent imagination will involve the introduction of ideas not specifically mentioned in the text. The question to be asked in such cases is: does the imagined sequence of events fit in naturally with the text or does it do violence to the text? In the present case, where the reconstruction is almost demanded by the text, I can see no difficulty at all.

13.　Mark records in chapter 8 a conversation of Jesus with his disciples about messiahship. He introduces it with the statement that 'Jesus and his disciples departed to the villages of Caesarea Philippi' (v.27). Schmidt concedes that these words follow on well from the previous story, the healing of the blind man at Bethsaida, since the distance between Bethsaida and Caesarea Philippi is about 40 km. But he argues that the two stories do not in fact belong together. His reason is that the question Jesus asks his disciples in verse 27: 'who do people say I am?' presupposes that the disciples are better informed than Jesus about what people are thinking. This conversation must therefore date from a period when Jesus had been separated from his disciples for some time – for example, the period when they went out on mission. It does not fit the context in which Mark has placed it because in chapter 8 Jesus is always in the company of his disciples. Mark is guilty of a discrepancy (*Unstimmigkeit*).[20]

This is an astonishing argument. Jesus regularly taught through question and answer. The theory that he asked questions only when the other person was better informed than himself would lead to curious results if consistently applied. It would mean that the crowd knew better than Jesus who his mother was (Mark 3:33), that the Pharisees knew better than Jesus whose head was on a Roman coin (Mark 12:16) and that the scribes knew better than Jesus who acted as neighbour to the man attacked by robbers (Luke 10:36). An instructive passage is Mark 9:33–37, in which Jesus asks a question, receives no answer, and then gives teaching which shows that he knew the answer anyway. Schmidt's argument illustrates his tendency to pedantic literalism – every statement and every question must be taken at its face value.

Conclusion

In this chapter we have been considering a mass of small details. Some of Schmidt's cricitisms of Mark have been shown to be fallacious, others merely petty. It would be easy to dismiss these criticisms as being of only marginal importance, since any writer who is breaking new ground, as Schmidt was, is bound to slip up here and there in point of detail. But it would be a great mistake to do this. The effect of Schmidt's work is cumulative – he piles up example after example of supposed Markan incompetence, and although many of his criticisms relate to minor details of interpretation their cumulative effect is considerable. Only by analysis of these individual criticisms can it be seen how inconclusive and, in many cases, how absurd so many of them are. The sheer volume of unsustainable arguments in Schmidt's book must create doubts about the validity of his overall thesis.

Notes

1 Schmidt, *Rahmen* 29.
2 E.V. Rieu (tr.) *The Odyssey* (Penguin, Harmondsworth 1946) 19.
3 *Rahmen* 308.
4 Ibid. 316, quoted in Chapter 2 n.27.
5 Ibid. 59f.
6 Ibid. 66.
7 Ibid. 84.
8 Ibid. 298.
9 Ibid. 101f.
10 Ibid. 69 (for the Sermon on the Mount) and 113 (for the Sermon on the Plain).
11 Ibid. 131:'4:1–9; 10–12; 13–20; 21–23; 24–25; 26–29; 30–32 are separate units, which have been placed side by side in a free and easy way (*zwanglos*).'
12 Ibid. 130.
13 Schmidt's other ground for accusing Mark of 'extreme unconcern about time and place' in this passage is related to the *argument from silence* and is discussed in the next chapter p. 52.
14 *Rahmen* 145.
15 Ibid. 151f. 'One must beware in such passages of overvaluing the Markan outline. Supporters of the Markan hypothesis tend to do this again and again, when they say that Matthew has placed Mark 5:21ff. in an inferior context. Let us put this to the test and ask some questions of our supposed chronologist Mark. Jesus preaches to the people (4:1ff.), in the evening or late afternoon of the same day he crosses over to the territory of the Gerasenes (4:35), having arrived there he heals a demoniac (5:1ff.), makes a return crossing, is called to Jairus's house, heals a woman on the way and in the house raises Jairus's daughter to life (5:21ff.). All this happened on one day. So a large part of the public ministry of Jesus as Mark portrays it took place on a single day. Since this is often held to be absurd, scholars are forced to begin by making deletions. Suspicion is cast on the words ὀψίας γενομένης (when it was evening) in 4:35, or a time interval is interposed between 5:20 and 5:21. These are attempts to escape from a dilemma, whose aim is to preserve as far as possible a chronological thread in Mark's gospel, and therefore they fail to do justice to the compositional technique of the second evangelist.'
16 Ibid. 152n.2.

17   Ibid. 164. For further discussion of Mark 6:30, see Chapter 12.

18   Ibid. 147: 'There is a problem involved in the naming of this name. Quite apart from the fact that the name Jairus is missing in D (Codex Bezae), it is remarkable that he is subsequently only referred to by his title (vv.35,38). That is stylistically not totally objection-free, isolates the mention of the name in v.22, and makes it not totally improbable that we have here an interpolation. A similar situation arises with the name Bartimaeus in 10:46 and the name Simon of Cyrene in 15:21. These names were already preserved in the tradition. In the present case also Mark will have found the name of Jairus already present in his source. But the stylistic issue we have referred to makes it probable that at some stage the name was added to the tradition. That additions of this sort occurred is shown by the story of the woman with the haemorrhage that is attached to the story of Jairus. As the Gospel of Nicodemus shows (Chapter 7), later legend gave to this woman the name Veronica. The formation of such legends may have begun in the very earliest period before the composition of our gospels.'

19   Ibid. 194f

20   Ibid. 215f.

4

The Argument from Silence

The argument from silence has always been a favourite argument with 'negative' scholars.[1] The fact that an evangelist fails to mention something the critic thinks he should have mentioned can lead to a variety of conclusions. Schmidt regards the 'silences' in the gospels as significant in three main respects: as indications of the fragmentary nature of the material; as indications of internal contradiction; and as indications of the editorial standpoint of the evangelist concerned.

i)   Silence and fragmentation

In Schmidt's opinion Mark's tradition consisted mainly of short independent pericopes. Only if the link between two pericopes is detailed and circumstantial does he take seriously the possibility that they were already connected at a pre-Markan stage. He employs the argument from silence as a means of proving that, wherever such detailed connecting links are absent, there was originally no connection at all.

   a)   Mark 1:16–20 relates the call of the four fishermen by the Sea of Galilee. In his commentary Schmidt declares that he will begin with a negative – with a statement of what is lacking in Mark's narrative. He points out that there is no chronological or topographical transition from the two preceding verses, which summarize Jesus's preaching ministry in Galilee. We are not told for how long or in what part of Galilee Jesus had been preaching up to this point, or by what route and from what place he came to the lake. Moreover, the names of Simon and Andrew are brought in without any introduction (just as John the Baptist's name was not properly introduced earlier in the chapter). For these deficiencies Schmidt has a straighforward explanation: Mark has simply reproduced his sources word for word. His sources, the storytellers, were telling the stories to an audience who already knew the details; and anyhow they were not interested in tracing the connections between different events, but only in isolated pericopes. So the question, for example, as to whether Simon and Andrew were already acquainted with Jesus or were here meeting him for the first time was not, in Schmidt's opinion, a question that would have concerned them.[2]

These comments are typical of Schmidt's use of the argument from silence. In his view, Mark is basically not an author but a copyist. If Mark fails to mention the chronological and topographical connections between events, this is not because, as a literary artist, he wanted to tell it that way, but because he was limited by the lack of information in his sources. It never seems to occur to Schmidt that authors can deliberately choose to be brief – that brevity is often more effective than prolixity and a fast-moving story is more readable than a story cumbered with a mass of background details.

It is interesting to compare Schmidt's approach with that of E.V. Rieu. In the introduction to his translation of the gospels, Rieu appraises Mark as follows:

> He has moulded his disconnected materials into a rapid, consecutive narrative which can best be praised in a very simple way by saying that once one has started reading it one cannot stop, and that however often it is read the spell remains. But it is much easier to feel these effects than to see how Mark secures them. He is certainly a master of detail. But he knows equally well where, for the sake of contrast, to omit it. A single sentence illustrates my meaning. 'Then they crucified him, and parcelled out his clothes, casting lots for them to see what each should have.' Four words for the crucifixion of Christ; fifteen for the men who had nailed him to the cross.[3]

The comments of Rieu and Schmidt represent two different approaches to literary criticism. Rieu tries to understand Mark's technique from a literary point of view. Schmidt's concern is with what the narrative would logically have required if it had been written in the style of a twentieth-century scholar.

b)   In 2:13–17 Mark relates three events: the call of Levi; a meal at Levi's house; and a subsequent conversation between some disciples of Jesus and some scribes and Pharisees. Schmidt aims to show that these were originally three independent stories. Because the stories are not provided with the logical connections of time and place he thinks they require, he concludes that originally they were not connected at all.[4]

His first objection is that the time at which the meal took place is not specified, which means in his view that that there is no proper connection between the call-story and the meal-story. This leads to the theory that verse 15 (the meal) marks the beginning of a new section, which originally had nothing to do with the story of Levi's call. I do not know what specification of time would satisfy Schmidt. Would 'three days later at 6.30 in the evening' be required, or would he be satisfied with 'three days later'? Suffice it to say that the difficulty does not lie in Mark's narrative (which is abbreviated but perfectly intelligible) but in the fact that Mark has not included a detail that Schmidt imagines he would have included if he had been writing the gospel himself.

Schmidt's second objection is to the abrupt appearance of the scribes and Pharisees in verse 16. We are not told when or where they approached the disciples. Was it during the meal or after the meal, or were they invited to the meal? Because of the absence of this information, and because the conversation in verses 16f. would make sense on its own, Schmidt argues that this conversation constituted an originally independent pericope which Mark has clumsily placed at this point.

In order to evaluate these objections, let us first imagine how Mark's narrative would read like if all the details Schmidt requires were included, beginning at the end of verse 14:

'. . . and Levi stood up and followed Jesus. Three days later Levi invited Jesus to a meal at his house at 6.30 pm. He invited many tax-collectors and sinners to the meal, and also a large number of disciples of Jesus. The meal took place in the courtyard of his house, which was open to public gaze. Some Pharisees who lived in Capernaum happened to be passing by and noticed the company Jesus was keeping. So next day at 10.30 in the morning they confronted some of the disciples in the market-place near to Ishmael's fruit and vegetable stall and asked them why Jesus ate with tax-collectors and sinners . . .'

If Mark had written this kind of circumstantial account, his narrative would have become so wordy that he would only have been able to include half the number of stories in the space available. But literary considerations of this sort do not concern Schmidt. For him Mark's silence is always a logical problem, not a literary one.

c)   After relating the parable of the sower (4:1–9) Mark continues in verse 10: 'When he was on his own, Jesus's companions (including the twelve) asked him about the parables.' Where, Schmidt asks, did this conversation take place? Was it in a house, on the road or by the sea? These are questions, he declares, that must be asked if we are to assume a continuous thread in Mark's presentation.[5] In other words, unless Mark records the precise sequence of events by which Jesus moves from Situation A to Situation B, and the precise location of Situation B, Schmidt's logic requires us to presume that Situations A and B were not originally connected.

It is not easy to grasp the reasoning behind this argument. The original sources of the stories of Jesus were the eyewitnesses. If Peter or one of the other apostles remembered asking Jesus a question about his teaching, would he necessarily remember the exact place where he asked it? More importantly, when telling groups of early Christians about his question and the reply he received, would he necessarily refer to the exact place even if he did remember it? The link between the question and the teaching that prompted it would be a necessary and important link in his mind; the link between the question and its exact location would seem incidental and unimportant. There are no grounds for Schmidt's assumption that the context of a story can be historical only if every unimportant detail is recorded.

Schmidt also poses the question: where do the companions of Jesus suddenly appear from in verse 10, when they were not named in verse 1?[6] Verse 1 refers to Jesus preaching to a large crowd. Schmidt implies that, because the disciples are not mentioned at this point, verse 1 and verse 10 must originally have belonged to different contexts. The logic behind this argument seems to be that, wherever Mark refers to Jesus preaching to a crowd, the disciples are not understood to be present unless they are specifically mentioned.

To show how ridiculous this argument is, let me give an example of how it might be used to discredit a modern newspaper report:

'The "Daily Clarion" in its issue of November 27th 1995 made two statements: (i) that on November 25th Oldcastle United defeated Whiteburn Rovers 3-0 in front of a crowd of 30,000 people; (ii) that when the Rovers' manager was asked for his comments after the match, he replied, "The mystery of football is known only to its players." There is a logical inconsistency in this report. Where did the manager suddenly appear from in the second statement when he was not mentioned in the first? Moreover, where exactly did this supposed interview take place – on the pitch, in the dressing room, or at the radio station? These deficiencies in the report suggest that the manager's comments were not originally made after this particular match, and that the "Daily Clarion", with its usual disregard for matters of time and place, has clumsily juxtaposed two independent news items.'

A modern media critic who argued in this way would be ridiculed. Why, then, should a New Testament scholar who argues in a similar way be credited with a serious contribution to scholarship?

d)   In his introduction to the eschatological discourse (13:1ff.) Mark refers to two conversations held at two separate locations – one in the temple and one on the Mount of Olives. Schmidt regards these as separate pericopes which Mark has artificially combined, and quotes a remark of Spitta's that the artificiality is confirmed by the absence of any motive for Jesus to go to the Mount of Olives.[7] This is a typical use of the argument from silence – no statement can be believed unless a motive is given for the action described. One wonders what would happen if this principle were applied in a court of law – if a police officer's introductory statement, 'I was proceeding along Market Street', were not admissible as evidence unless a motive for proceeding along Market Street were also provided.

The four examples I have quoted all illustrate the same scholarly technique. If a story lacks the precise details of time, place or motive that Schmidt thinks it requires, this is taken as proof that Mark had no idea of its original context and has placed it in its present location for schematic reasons. Three comments are appropriate.

First, the list of Markan omissions is Schmidt's personal list. In effect he is saying, 'If I had written Mark's gospel myself, these are the things I should have mentioned.'[8]

Second, Schmidt's list reflects an academic historical approach rather than a literary approach. The fact that Mark's gospel is read today by millions of people all over the world is a testimony to the soundness of his literary judgment in omitting inessential facts and presenting a fast-moving, exciting narrative. The stories in Mark's gospel are similar to the line drawings by Annie Vallotton that illustrate many editions of the Good News Bible: basic sketches in black and white, which leave the filling in of details to the imagination of the reader.

Third, Schmidt takes no account of the pressure of space and the need to abbreviate which form such an important feature of popular literature. This pressure is not felt to the same extent in the case of academic literature, which can still get published even if it lengthy to the point of being boring. That is one reason why the judgments of academic scholars on a author such as Mark often show a lack of understanding of his situation.

ii)   Silence and contradiction

Schmidt's second use of the *argument from silence* is to prove internal contradictions in a particular gospel. His implicit assumption seems to be that each evangelist aimed to provide comprehensive coverage of the ministry of Jesus, so that any event not recorded did not, in that evangelist's view, take place. Therefore, if it is implied elsewhere in that gospel that such an event did take place, this constitutes an internal contradiction.

In the light of the condensed and abbreviated nature of the gospels, this is a very strange argument. All the evangelists could have echoed the words of John (21:25) that if everything Jesus did were written down, the whole world could not contain the books that would be written. They coped with this problem in two ways: by the device of summary statements (*Sammelberichte*) covering long periods in a few words; and by a paradigmatic style of presentation in which each recorded event represented a multitude of similar unrecorded events. However, Schmidt does not consider the silence of the evangelists from a literary point of view. For him silence is a logical problem, not a literary one. Let us look at two examples of his approach.

a)   In the story of the meal at Levi's house (2:13–17) Mark states that by this time Jesus had a large number of followers. Where did all these disciples come from, Schmidt asks, since so far in the gospel the only disciples to be called are the four fishermen? He sees this problem as a confirmation of his view that the meal-story did not originally belong to the same context as the preceding story of Levi's call.[9]

Schmidt's objection fails to appreciate the paradigmatic technique of Mark's gospel. The only way Mark could condense the ministry of Jesus into a small compass was by giving a representative sample only of each activity of Jesus. Mark's original readers would not have expected, as Schmidt seems to expect, that the call of each individual apostle should be separately recorded.

b)   In Matthew's account of the healing of the centurion's servant (8:5–13) Jesus comments that he had not found even in Israel such faith as the centurion's. Schmidt objects that up to this point Matthew has related so little of the ministry of Jesus that Jesus would not have had the opportunity to test how much faith the Israelites had. He therefore concludes that the story belongs to a later stage in the ministry of Jesus than Matthew has assigned to it.[10] The implication seems to be that, if we take Matthew literally, the only people Jesus had met prior to his conversation with the centurion were the people Matthew specifically mentions as having met him.

This argument is not only odd in itself; it runs contrary to the evidence. Several chapters earlier (4:23–25) Matthew refers to an extensive preaching and healing tour through the whole of Galilee, which attracted crowds from Galilee, Decapolis, Jerusalem, Judaea and Peraea. Schmidt is probably right to regard 4:23–25 as an introductory summary to chapters 5 to 9, so that the story of the centurion's servant forms part of the Galilee ministry there summarized.[11] He is certainly right to say that summaries of this kind cannot be made the basis of a precise chronology.[12] We do not in fact know how many weeks or months 4:23–25 was intended by Matthew to cover. But this uncertainty undermines Schmidt's argument. If the healing of the centurion's servant took place at some unspecified point in an extensive preaching and healing tour throughout Galilee, we have no means of knowing how many Israelites Jesus had met during that time whose faith could be compared with that of the centurion.

c) I conclude this section with a cautionary tale. In his discussion of Mark 2:23–28 (the story of the disciples plucking ears of corn) Schmidt points out that this event must have happened at harvest time soon after the Passover. Since Mark refers to one Passover only, various scholars before Schmidt had concluded that the ministry of Jesus lasted for only one year.[13] According to this theory the corn-plucking episode must have occurred during harvest time in the year previous to the first Easter. Schmidt, on the contrary, argues that there is no chronological framework at all in Mark, and therefore the assumption of a one-year ministry is pure hypothesis (*ein blosses Postulat*); the most we can deduce from the corn-plucking episode, he declares, is that the ministry of Jesus must have lasted for a *minimum* of one year. This is an important point, since the various events related in Mark could have taken place within the space of three to five months. Therefore, Schmidt concludes, 'had this story not been in the tradition, a duration of a few months for the ministry of Jesus would, on the basis of Mark's gospel, have been regarded as an assured historical fact.'[14]

Let us look at this statement more closely. It represents Schmidt's assessment of what scholars of that period would have been bound to do, had this chance allusion to an earlier harvest not been recorded. It thus pinpoints the scholarly methods which (at least in Schmidt's opinion) were prevalent at the time. Two assumptions in particular seem to underlie the few-month theory.

1)   The assumption that John's gospel (which implies at least a three-year ministry) is to be discounted where it conflicts with the supposed chronology of Mark. This assumption was regularly made in his day, Schmidt tells us,[15] though it did not of course represent the view of the 'harmonizers' (such as the 'Catholic exegetes' lambasted in footnotes throughout the book) whose error was to regard John and Mark as complementary rather than contradictory.

2)   The assumption that the *argument from silence* is a reputable scholarly argument. Only on this assumption can one argue that Mark's failure to refer to more than one passover in the ministry of Jesus is equivalent to a positive statement that there only was one.

Schmidt is quite right to reject the argument from silence in this instance, and to point out that its devotees had been saved from a major blunder only by a chance reference to an earlier harvest. It is unfortunate that he does not follow through the logic of his own criticism and reject the argument from silence more radically.

iii)   Silence and design

One of the curiosities of the argument from silence is the way its devotees feel they have to provide an explanation for every omission. Wherever Matthew or Luke fail to record something that is in Mark, some reason for this omission must be produced. For example, Matthew does not record the story of the widow's mite. Schmidt admits that it is difficult to find a reason for the omission, but this does not deter him from trying. The fact that this story would not fit easily into Matthew's narrative at the corresponding place to Mark 12 (Matthew chapters 23 to 25) does not explain why Matthew has not found a place for it elsewhere in the gospel. Schmidt therefore suggests the possibility that this story, with its 'Lukan' emphasis on women and poverty, may have been taken from Luke and interpolated into the Markan text.[16] He also reads a significance into Luke's omission of any reference to Bethany in the days before the passion , which indicates, in his opinion, that Luke thinks Jesus stayed in Jerusalem the whole time.[17] On the other hand, the fact that Luke omits the mockery of Jesus by the soldiers does not seem to him to be significant or to suggest lack of hostoricity. Luke, he comments, will have had 'some grounds or other' for the omission, and he quotes in a footnote some attempts by Johannes Weiss to guess Luke's motives.[18]

I wonder why he could not have remained equally vague about the reasons for the other omissions. As I have argued elsewhere,[19] the art of omission is an important element in the art of writing, and the factors predisposing an author to include Item A and omit Item B are so many and so complicated that a scholar has little chance of guessing them right nineteen centuries later.

A case in point is Mark 3:6 and its parallel in Luke 6:11. According to Mark the Pharisees plotted with the Herodians as to how to kill Jesus. Luke does not mention the Herodians or talk of killing – the Pharisees and teachers of the law discuss among themselves 'what they might do to Jesus'. The reason for these omissions, according to Schmidt, is obvious. Luke thinks that talk of a murder plot at this stage in Jesus's ministry is premature. When he does mention a murder plot later on (13:31) the situation is different, and the Pharisees are playing off Herod against Jesus.[20]

In my opinion the reasons for one evangelist omitting what another includes are rarely obvious. Here is another possible reason – conjectural, like Schmidt's, and therefore of equal validity to his. There is no mention of the Herodians anywhere in Luke. His gospel was dedicated to a Roman official and intended for Gentile readers, and he may have felt that the Herodians would mean nothing to his audience, and ignored them for that reason. Moreover, though it is true that Luke 6:11 does not specifically mention killing, this may well be implied by the statement that the Pharisees, being out of their mind with anger, were discussing 'what they might do to Jesus' (τί ἄν ποιήσαιεν τίῷ Ἰησοῦ).[21] Luke uses a similar phrase in a context of murder in the parable of the vineyard and its tenants: 'What will the owner of the vineyard do to them? (τί οὖν ποιήσει αὐτοῖς ὁ κύριος τοῦ ἀμπελῶνος;) He will come and kill those tenants.'(20:15f.) Schmidt's view that Luke has deliberately weakened Mark's account

for chronological reasons is a guess, and no more likely to be correct
than any other guess.

Notes

1   For a discussion of the argument from silence in the New Testament in general,
    see my *Seven Pillories* Chapter 4 pp.55–64.
2   Schmidt, *Rahmen* 43f.
3   E.V. Rieu, *The Four Gospels* (Penguin, Harmondsworth 1952)xxi.
4   *Rahmen* 82–6.
5   Ibid. 130.
6   Ibid.
7   Ibid. 287 n.1.
8   In this respect, C.S. Lewis had a feeling of sympathy for the gospel writers, based
    on his experience of having his books reviewed. His critics, he had found, often
    tried to read into his mind their own attributes. 'They assume that you wrote a
    story as they would try to write a story; the fact that they would so try explains
    why they have not produced any stories. But are the Biblical critics in this way
    much better off?. . . .' (C.S. Lewis, *Christian Reflections*, Collins, Glasgow 1981)
    202.
9   *Rahmen* 84.
10 Ibid. 74.
11 Ibid. 69.
12 Ibid. 68.
13 For an example of such an argument by Albert Schweitzer see below p. 143f.
14 *Rahmen* 90f. 'There is still far too much effort made to hold on somehow to the
    Markan framework in particular, and that framework is corrected as sparingly
    as possible. By contrast, our investigation up to this point has shown that, strictly
    speaking, Mark has no framework and no outline. Separate stories are arranged
    in a loose order, some with statements of time and place, some without. It is
    pure hypothesis to assume that because of the Passover the various narratives
    should be distributed over a maximum of one year. . . . Where the fact of this
    harvest deserves our gratitude is in showing that the Synoptic stories of Jesus
    should be distributed over a minimum of one year. Had this story not been in
    the tradition, an actual duration of a few months for the ministry of Jesus would,
    on the basis of Mark's gospel, have been regarded as an assured historical fact.'
15 Ibid. 91. 'The attempts to regard the chronology of John's Gospel as authentic
    and integrate it with the synoptic framework in a harmonising way are not to be
    rejected on the grounds, for example, that they do violence to the synoptic (i.e.
    the Markan) outline. This criticism, which is the one normally directed against
    the advocates of such harmonistic efforts, is not the correct one. The three-year
    Johannine chronology, which has much to be said for it on psychological
    grounds over against the well-loved one-year theory, should rather be subjected
    to its own literary evaluation before being accepted as historical.'
16 Ibid. 277.
17 Ibid. 298.

18 Ibid. 307. 'The fact that the same evangelist does not mention the mockery of
    Jesus by the Roman soldiers does not prove at all that this episode did not
    originally belong to its present context. At this point Luke will have had some
    grounds or other for leaving out one piece of the authentic passion story.'
19 Hall, *Seven Pillories* 61–4.
20 Ibid. 103. 'If the well-known opponents of Jesus, the scribes and Pharisees, are
    named, why is there no mention of the Herodians? The closing sentence gives
    us a clue: αὐτοὶ δὲ ἐπλήσθησαν ἀνοίας, καὶ διελάλουν πρὸς ἀλλήλους τί ἂν
    ποιήσαιεν τῷ Ἰησοῦ. In Mark the talk is of murder plots. Luke weakens this.
    His reasons are obvious. He thinks this murder plan is premature. Only later
    does he speak clearly of such a conspiracy in 13:31, and there it is Herod himself
    who is played off against Jesus by the Pharisees. Thus it is the pragmatism of
    Luke's presentation, a chronological consideration, that has caused him to make
    an alteration in this passage.'
21 The phrase ἐπλήσθησαν ἀνοίας (they were filled with frenzy), which is peculiar
    to Luke, scarcely suggests a 'weakening' of the Markan original.

5

The Argument from Textual Tradition

A considerable portion of Schmidt's book is devoted to discussion of textual variants. This serves two purposes – to establish the best text; and to draw from the variant readings conclusions about the pre-history of the text.

i) Establishing the Text

Schmidt's approach to textual criticism can perhaps best be described as eclectic. There is little attempt to evaluate the manuscripts according to age or provenance. On occasion, he seems to choose the reading that best suits his argument. Here are two examples.

a) The saying in Luke 10:22 in some manuscripts lacks any introductory statement, but in other manuscripts is introduced with the words: 'and Jesus turned to his disciples and said . . .' These words are almost identical with the words used to introduce the saying in the following verse (v. 23). Schmidt prefers the longer reading in verse 22, and argues that those manuscript scribes who omitted these words did so deliberately because they were repeated in the following verse and were felt to be intrusive. At the same time he mentions the fact that important manuscripts (XBDL) support the shorter reading.[1]

Schmidt has, of course, every right to express a personal preference in a disputed issue. The problem is that two pages later he uses the reading he prefers as the basis of his argument to demonstrate what he believes to be Luke's editorial technique. His theory is that Luke took over unaltered the introductions to the pericopes that he found in his sources:

The fact that Luke is dependent on the pericope-introductions that lay to hand is demonstrated in a graphic way by 10:22 and 10:23, where two references to Jesus speaking to his disciples follow each other closely. In v. 23 this reference is completely superfluous. Understandably later copyists have tried to remedy this by omitting v. 22a.[2]

The fact that the repetition of these words is superfluous and awkward is obvious to everyone. What is not obvious is Schmidt's explanation. According to his theory Luke copied this phrase word for word from his source in both cases, and was presumably either too unobservant to notice the awkward repetition or too lazy to care. Schmidt repeatedly lays similar charges against Mark, whom he regards as a clumsy and unintelligent copyist. But he describes Luke as 'a clever author,' who makes all sorts of stylistic improvements to the Markan text.[3] An awkward repetition of this sort would be out of character for Luke in the light of Schmidt's own evaluation.

Quite apart from that, however, the main problem with Schmidt's argument here is his total dependence on a doubtful textual variant. It is illegitimate to treat such a variant as though it were the established text and make deductions from it in this way.

b) In Chapter 9 Mark records the healing of an epileptic boy immediately after the transfiguration. Schmidt concedes that the two stories fit well together, but is still able to discover a difficulty. Some manuscripts have singular verbs in verse 14 (and *he* (Jesus) came to the disciples and saw a great crowd); other manuscripts have plural verbs (and *they* came and saw a great crowd). According to Schmidt the singular is probably the correct reading, and the use of a singular verb indicates that Jesus had been somewhere on his own. This does not suit the Markan context of the descent from the mount of transfiguration, since on that occasion Jesus was accompanied by three disciples.[4]

In this case Schmidt does not, as in the previous instance, treat his personal preference for one form of the text as though it were proven fact. He admits that the reading he prefers was rejected by the majority of scholars in his day (as it has been rejected by the majority of scholars ever since). But he nevertheless devotes a whole page to the advocacy of this reading, and to promoting the thesis that, if this reading is adopted, the good connection with the preceding narrative goes out of the window. This seems a surprising weight of argument to rest upon such a doubtful variant. Perhaps the lack of any alternative means of casting doubt on the connection between the two stories forced Schmidt to do this.

What makes Schmidt's argument so strange is the fact that, even if the singular verbs do represent the original text, the connection between the stories is still perfectly good. Mark's account of the transfiguration ends with a conversation between Jesus and the three disciples as they come down from the mountain. The disciples' question in verse 11 is followed by Jesus's reply in verses 12,13. Thus a singular verb in verse 14 would not create any ambiguity, since the subject would be the same as the subject of the two preceding verses. Moreover, Jesus is often referred to in the singular in Mark when disciples are also present. For example, in 2:23 we read that he (Jesus) was walking through some cornfields and his disciples began to pluck ears of corn. If the use of the singular is taken to imply that Jesus was on his own, there is a logical problem here; but in his commentary on 2:23 Schmidt makes no mention of such a problem. He assumes, as does everyone else, that Mark refers to Jesus in the singular because he is the main character in the story, even though Mark and all his readers are aware that disciples are present. In practice, the assumption that the use of the singular implies that Jesus is on his own is made by Schmidt only when it suits his purpose to make it.

ii)   Textual variants and gospel tradition

The importance of textual criticism is not limited in Schmidt's eyes to the establishment of the best text. He believes that a study of the methodology of later copyists, even where it is agreed that their alterations do not constitute the original text, can provide clues to the factors at work at an earlier stage in the tradition. There are two features of the later manuscripts in particular that interest him : 'pericope praxis' and attempts to improve the context.

a)   One of the characteristics of the later manuscripts was what Schmidt calls 'pericope praxis' – the division of the gospels into independent units for lectionary purposes. For instance, if a story in Mark began with the words 'and he entered Capernaum', this could be altered to 'Jesus entered Capernaum', so that when the passage was read in church it would be immediately intelligible. Schmidt accepts that these readings do not represent the original text of Mark's gospel; but he thinks they do provide hints as to the original form of the pericopes in the pre-Markan tradition.[5]

There are, on this theory, three stages in the tradition: 1) independent pericopes in oral tradition; 2) combined narratives in the written gospels; 3) independent pericopes in church lectionaries and in manuscripts influenced by lectionaries. The third stage is seen as a reversion to type, eliminating the artificial merger of the independent pericopes by the evangelists. That is why the attempts of later scribes to re-isolate the pericopes are said to provide valuable hints as to their original form.

A good example of this argument is Schmidt's discussion of Mark 6:34. According to Mark 6:30–33 the apostles came to Jesus after their preaching mission and told him what they had done; he said they needed some rest, so they went in a boat to a desert place, and the crowd saw them go and came by land to the same place. Finally (v. 34) Jesus got out of the boat, began to teach them and eventually fed five thousand people. The narrative reads smoothly and continuously. But Schmidt points out that many manuscripts add the name of Jesus in verse 34, so that instead of 'he left the boat' we have 'Jesus left the boat'. The addition of the name of Jesus at the start of a story is, as he says, a common feature of the manuscripts, which he correctly attributes to 'pericope praxis' and the influence of lectionaries. But in the present case he cites this textual variant as evidence in support of the view that 6:34 marks the beginning of a new, originally independent pericope. Such a view, he argues, would be in accordance with Mark's literary technique as it has been elucidated earlier in the book: the feeding story is understandable on its own, and it is in the nature of such isolated stories that the main characters – the crowd and the disciples – are simply present without being specially introduced. He concludes: 'This makes it clear once again that 6:30–33 is a unit on its own, which must be separated from 6:34ff.'[6]

This discussion is a good example of what counts in Schmidt's eyes as a logical argument. His conclusion reads like a logical necessity – 6:30–33 *must* be separated from 6:34. But the evidence does not remotely justify this. Schmidt has indeed argued in many places earlier in the book that Mark has combined originally independent pericopes; but in a few places he has admitted that some pericopes were already linked in the tradition. Which of these two situations applies in the present case we have no means of proving. The feeding of the five thousand *could*, as Schmidt says, stand on its own without the background information of the preceding verses; but that does not mean that it *did*. That information makes the feeding story more intelligible, and it is difficult to see why verses 31–33 should have been composed by Mark out of his own head, as Schmidt believes. The only positive argument Schmidt adduces for the separation of verse 33 from verse 34 is the textual evidence: the fact that later copyists added the name of Jesus, and thus enabled verses 34ff. to be separated off as a lectionary reading in Christian worship, makes a similar separation in Mark's sources a logical necessity!

b) The tendency of 'pericope praxis' was to isolate pericopes; but there was also a tendency working in the opposite direction. When copying manuscripts scribes tried to make the narrative hold together better by adding connecting particles and explanatory phrases. An example is the addition in some manuscripts of the word πάλιν (again) in Mark 11:15, when Jesus enters Jerusalem for the second time after having entered it on the previous day (11:11). When such scribal alterations occur in the text of Mark, Schmidt regards them as indicative of the loose structure of that gospel: scribes felt it necessary to correct Mark because he so often juxtaposed independent units of tradition without properly assimilating them.[7] In the case of Luke, the improvements made by later scribes are thought to be comparable to the improvements made by Luke himself to his source material. According to Schmidt, Luke had to organize and bring into order a multitude of separate stories, and the scribes had to deal with Luke in a similar way. On the one hand, Luke had not gone far enough in creating a running narrative out of his disparate material; on the other hand, when the scribes wished to re-isolate the pericopes, there was too much background material in Luke. Therefore the manuscript tradition is highly instructive (*äusserst instruktiv*) in helping us to discover the distinctive nature of the third gospel.[8]

This comparison between Luke and the later scribes is dependent on Schmidt's theory that Luke used only one source at a time – that where he is dependent on Mark he follows Mark alone, and is thus in a similar position to a scribe copying a single manuscript. But even so it seems exaggerated to say that the manuscript tradition is 'highly instructive' in determining the nature of Luke's gospel. The most we can say, even on Schmidt's presuppositions, is that later copyists faced a somewhat similar situation to Luke's and that Luke *could* have worked on the same principles as they did. Whether he in fact *did* work on those principles can be determined only by examining Luke's original text (insofar as we can establish it).

iii)   The supposed use of Mark by Matthew and Luke

Schmidt regards the priority of Mark as a proven fact and thinks of Matthew and Luke as editors of, and thus commentators upon, the Markan text. In his view the 'alterations' of Mark by Matthew and Luke are on the same level as the alterations made by later manuscript scribes and can teach us similar lessons. These lessons include the loose structure of the Markan original (which made these alterations both necessary and easy to make) and the supposed motives of Matthew and Luke in making their alterations.

In his overview of the Markan section 10:46–13:37, Schmidt discusses the parallels to this section in Matthew and Luke. He treats these under four headings: omissions made by Matthew and Luke; their interpolations; their transpositions; and their remodelling of the pericope introductions. In each case, he regards these procedures as deliberate alteration of the Markan original, for editorial and stylistic reasons, and also, in Luke's case, in the interests of periodizing and psychologizing.[9] He does not recognize the possibility that Matthew or Luke could have had other sources of information (whether oral or written) which they combined with Mark to form a new synthesis.

For example, Luke records immediately after the triumphal entry that Jesus wept over Jerusalem and uttered a prophecy of its destruction (19. 41–44). Spitta, an advocate of Lukan priority, had argued that the contrast between the popular acclamation at the triumphal entry and this sad prophecy is so natural that one cannot conceive of its being a later addition. Schmidt's view is diametrically opposed. He suggests three possible reasons for Luke to introduce the prophecy at this point. a) Luke is deliberately paving the way for the prophecy of Jerusalem's destruction in Chapter 21 by showing that Jesus knew before he entered the city about its final end. b) The contrast between the acclamation of the people and the grief of Jesus is psychologically effective because Luke was an expert at such psychological features. c) The reference to stones crying out in 19:40 may have reminded Luke of the saying about not one stone remaining on another.[10] The one possibility Schmidt does not take seriously is that the prophecy could have been already set in its present context in one of Luke's other sources.

Schmidt's one-track approach to Luke's 'alterations' raises a number of issues. One is the much-debated question as to how far the relationships between the gospels are literary and how far they are

oral. At the 1977 colloquy on the gospels at San Antonio there was
an exchange of views on this issue between Albert B. Lord and Charles
H. Talbert. Lord argued that the synoptic texts vary from one another
to such an extent as to rule out the possibility that, as a whole, one
could have been copied from another, and attributes the differences
to 'an oral traditional relationship among the texts'. Talbert argued
that copying other people's work with variations was a recognized
literary procedure in the ancient world, and quoted examples from
Josephus and others.[11] Arguments can be adduced in favour of either
view, and it may be that we need to combine the insights of both. So
far as the relationship of Matthew and Luke with Mark is concerned,
however, Schmidt's exclusive reliance on a theory of deliberate literary
alteration appears questionable for two reasons.

First, much of Schmidt's argument depends on his familiar technique of turning possibilities into facts. We have referred earlier to his
repeated declaration that Luke did not 'need' a special source for his
additional information, and therefore did not have one.[12] Luke's
additions are then credited to his clever deductions from the context
(e.g. the reference to Jairus' 'only' daughter[13], the mention of
Bethsaida in 9:10[14], and the reference to the Mount of Olives in
19:37).[15] In the case of Matthew, Schmidt makes an interesting
comment on the statement peculiar to Matthew that the rich ruler
who asked Jesus about eternal life was young (19:20,22). Schmidt
asks whether this statement indicates that Matthew had a separate
tradition, and replies that Matthew could have deduced the age of the
man from two elements in the story – the allusion to the fourth
commandment (honour your father and mother) and the rich ruler's
assertion in Mark 10:20 (and in some manuscripts of Matthew 19:20)
that he had kept the commandments 'from his youth'. Schmidt
concedes that neither of these factors justify any deduction as to the
man's age, but clearly feels that crediting Matthew with an unjustified
deduction from the Markan text is preferable to admitting the possibility that Matthew could have had supplementary sources of information.[16] The denial of such a possibility, in all the cases quoted, is a
matter not of evidence but of dogma.

Second, Luke refers in his preface to the many people who had
recounted the events of the life of Jesus before him. This suggests that,
if we accept Markan priority, Mark's gospel will have been one of
Luke's sources, but one among many. It is in any case difficult to
believe that Luke was totally ignorant of the ministry of Jesus until he

read Mark. More probably, as John Wenham has argued, Luke was already used to telling the stories of Jesus before Mark was written. Wenham summarizes his approach as follows:

> The later evangelists are seen as probably writing with knowledge of the earlier gospels – adopting the newly invented genre and in the main following the same order. But they are not seen as systematically altering their predecessors' work. . . . What they write is fundamentally what they themselves are accustomed to teach. So it is a case of some degree of structural dependence and a high degree of verbal independence.[17]

If we assume some kind of literary relationship between any two of the gospels, the differences between them can be explained in either of two ways: *either* the work of the earlier evangelist was the sole source of the later evangelist, so that every difference between them must be the result of deliberate alteration; *or* the later evangelist had received information about the life of Jesus from a variety of sources of which the earlier gospel was only one, and brought all this information together into a new integrated account. The latter view seems to me far more probable, though there is no way of logically demonstrating its truth. As Wenham says, it is difficult to see Matthew's gospel as the result of making eight thousand alterations to someone else's work, but it is not impossible.[18] The important thing is to note the extent of Schmidt's dependence on an unproved assumption. Once the conjectural nature of this assumption is recognized, his attempt to treat the 'alterations' in Matthew and Luke as on a par with the alterations of a manuscript scribe falls to the ground.

Notes

1 Schmidt, *Rahmen* 256.
2 Ibid. 258.
3 Ibid. 316.
4 Ibid. 228.
5 Ibid. 256 (referring to the text of the Lukan Travel Narrative) 'The fact that the text has been influenced by Pericope Praxis is clearly shown by the interpolation of the words ὁ Ἰησοῦς which has occurred in one manuscript or another in almost every introductory passage that refers to Jesus simply as "he" (e.g. 10:21; 11:5; 11:14; 11:37; 13:10 . . . 13:22; 15:1).' See also p. 276 (referring to alterations in the Markan text because of Pericope Praxis): 'The external attestation in these cases is not strong enough for these readings to represent the original text of Mark's gospel. However, the variant readings we have

quoted, which have arisen from Pericope Praxis, give a hint (*Fingerzeig*) of the original text of the separate pericopes as Mark received them from the tradition.'

6 Ibid. 190f.
7 Ibid. 275.
8 Ibid. 257.
9 Ibid. 277–287.
10 Ibid. 278f.
11 William O. Walker (ed) *The Relationships among the Gospels: an Interdisciplinary Dialogue* (San Antonio TX, Trinity University Press, 1978) 33–102.
12 See Chapter Two pp. 26–9.
13 *Rahmen* 148.
14 Ibid. 190.
15 Ibid. 298n.
16 Ibid. 242f.
17 John Wenham, *Redating Matthew, Mark and Luke* (Hodder and Stoughton, London, 1991) xxiii.
18 Ibid. 94.

6

The Argument from Literary Criticism

One of Schmidt's key principles is that literary criticism must take precedence over historical criticism. He accuses upholders of the Markan hypothesis, such as J. Weiss and Wellhausen, of overvaluation of the Markan historical outline. In his opinion Spitta had provided a much-needed corrective by pointing out the historical value of Luke and John; but Spitta also was guilty of forming a literary judgment from purely historical considerations. According to Schmidt the correct procedure is not to set one gospel off against another, but to examine the Markan framework on its own terms; and this can be done only by literary-critical investigation of individual units. It is this investigation that he sets as his own agenda.[1]

Schmidt's conception of literary criticism is quite different from the modern one. He thinks of Mark not as a creative author but as a copyist. He therefore does not seek to explain features of the text by reference to Mark's artistic feeling and literary skill. For Schmidt literary criticism is essentially disintegrative. It consists in the division of the gospel text into its constituent parts, and the application of a number of set criteria in order to decide the literary origin of each individual element. In this chapter we shall examine three of these criteria: the criterion of detachability; the criterion of characteristic words; and the criterion of multiple context.

i) The criterion of detachability

The theory behind the criterion of detachability is as follows: if a word or verse or whole pericope can be detached from its context in such a way that the words preceding and the words following fit in with each other, this suggests that the detachable element did not originally belong to its present context.

A good example is Mark 2:1 : 'and he [Jesus] entered Capernaum again after some time and news got around that he was in the house.'[2] Schmidt argues that Mark took the story that follows (the healing of the paralyzed man) from the tradition along with its introduction, but that the introduction as Mark received it simply said, 'and he was in the house'. The reference to entering Capernaum, on this theory, was added by Mark because he understood the house to be Peter's house in Capernaum, already mentioned in 1:29; and the reference to news getting around that he was in the house was added by Mark to fit in with the statement in the previous verse (1:45) that Jesus could no longer enter a town openly because of the crowds.[3]

The reason Schmidt provides for this theory is that the reference to the house is the only element in 2:1 that is necessary for understanding the ensuing narrative. The other statements of time and place are not 'anchored in the narrative itself' – the narrative does not lose anything if they are detached, and they have been added to fill the lacuna between chapters 1 and 2.

The principle lying behind this argument seems to be this: any detail in a story that is not required by the story, and that can therefore be detached without damage to the story, is to be attributed to the evangelist, not to the tradition. The implication is that the original eyewitnesses, to whom Schmidt believes the tradition does ultimately go back, would not have mentioned the location of any event unless the event could only have happened at that location; or if they did mention it, subsequent storytellers would have forgotten it by the time it reached Mark. So the only indications of time and place that could have survived the period of oral transmission are those that are essential to the story.

A modern parallel may help us to evaluate this scholarly principle. My friend John returns from a holiday in Greece and tells me something that happened to him in Athens. As I hear the story, I realize that this event could just as easily have happened in Corinth, which he also visited. Do I therefore doubt his statement that it happened in Athens? And if I think his story to be such a good one that I tell it to another friend, do I say, 'John told me an interesting thing that happened to him in Athens', or do I automatically omit the reference to Athens because the Athens location is not essential to the story? Or does my friend say to me, 'That cannot have happened in Athens, because the Athens location is not anchored in the narrative?' It seems to me that there is no rule of thumb, no law of tradition in these matters.

Of course, if we accept the possibility that the early church was right and that Mark got much of his information directly from Peter, the likelihood of Peter remembering the location of something that happened in his home town is extremely high. But even if, with Schmidt, we reject that even as a possibility, there are no grounds for his assumption that early church storytellers were incapable of transmitting the location of any event unless the event could have happened only at that location.

Sometimes a whole story is regarded as detachable. For example Schmidt finds two difficulties in the chronology of the account of the cleansing of the temple. The first is a discrepancy between Mark and Matthew. In Mark the order of events is: 1) the triumphal entry 2) retirement to Bethany for the night 3) the cursing of the fig-tree next morning 4) the cleansing of the temple 5) retirement to Bethany for the second night 6) discussion of the withering of the fig-tree next morning. In Matthew the order is: 1) the triumphal entry 2) the cleansing of the temple 3) retirement to Bethany 4) the cursing of the fig-tree next morning 5) discussion of the withering of the fig-tree immediately after its cursing. Schmidt describes Matthew's account as 'more an abbreviation than a transposition' of the Markan narrative, but regards it as highly significant for our evaluation of Mark's order that it could be changed at such an early stage without any damage to the overall context.[4]

The second difficulty is the fact that John places the cleansing of the temple early in his gospel – in the second chapter. Schmidt quotes the views of contemporary scholars who argued for an early or a late cleansing on psychological grounds, and objects that these arguments are irrelevant because the temple cleansing would have been appropriate at any stage in Jesus's ministry. His conclusion is that, in the gospel tradition, this story was not fixed at any particular time, and each evangelist was free to place it at any point he liked to fit in with his plan.[5]

Schmidt's claim that the psychological arguments cancel each other out seems to me to be justified. Scholars have to exercise their literary judgment in deciding whether, at this point, the various evangelists are being guided by schematic or chronological considerations. In the forming of this judgment, the criterion of detachability seems to me to be just as irrelevant as the psychological argument. A modern example illustrates this.

Suppose I hear separate reports of a football game from two friends. One of them describes how he saw one player score a goal, and then tells me that another player suffered an injury. My other friend relates the same two events, but describes the injury first and the goal later. If I want to know in which order these two events took place, and my friends are no longer available for questioning, I could try to remember whether either of them claimed to be relating the events in chronological order, or whether either of them had a special reason (such as personal friendship with the player concerned) for mentioning one event before the other. I should not assume from the bare fact that the events are easily transposable that the witnesses were confusing two separate football games, or that neither of them had any idea of the true sequence of events. Rather, I should assume that one or other of them had got the order right, even if I could not work out for certain which of them it was.

Schmidt himself recognizes the weakness of the criterion of detachability. He notes that the three passion predictions in Mark (8:31ff.,9:30ff.,10:32ff.) can all be smoothly detached from their contexts, and comments that this observation has less force because of Mark's paratactic style. For this reason, he concludes, our literary judgment of these predictions must depend on our evaluation of their content.[6] In similar vein he observes that Mark 1:23–28 could have been originally an independent pericope, and that if it is detached verses 22 and 29 fit well together, but continues: 'It is a fairly easy operation to detach units of material in this way, given the strictly paratactic nature of Mark's style. But this very fact warns us to be cautious and restrained.'[7]

This is a fair comment, and applies to many other passages as well. A paratactic style places a whole series of sayings and events side by side, like packets of seeds displayed for sale in a shop. If one variety of seeds is sold out, the packets to either side of it will probably still belong 'logically' together. Similarly in Mark virtually any pericope could be detached from its context without affecting the logical progression of the narrative. But this fact in itself is of no more significance than the detachability of a seed packet in a shop. Authors such as Mark who write in a paratactic style can arrange their material wholly chronologically (as upholders of the Markan hypothesis tended to believe) or wholly schematically (as Schmidt tended to believe) or partly chronologically and partly schematically. If we accept this third possibility, the judgment as to whether Mark's presentation is chronological or schematic must be decided in each case on its merits, and the criterion of detachability cannot be rolled out like a *deus ex machina* to decide the issue for us.

An illustration of Schmidt's ambivalence with regard to the criterion of detachability is his discussion of Mark 10:35–45. He notes that the request of James and John for the top places in the Kingdom of God (vv. 35–37) could be followed equally well by verses 38–40 or by verses 41–45, and that either of these two latter sections could be smoothly detached from Mark's narrative. He is undecided as to which of the two should be detached (he does not consider the possibility that they might both belong to the same context) and comments:

> With Mark's paratactic style of presentation it is methodologically interesting how easily verses and groups of verses can be detached from their context, and there is always the danger of dividing to death (*sich tot zu teilen*).[8]

It is unfortunate that Schmidt, being well aware of this danger, falls into it so often.

ii) The criterion of characteristic words

The theory behind the criterion of characteristic words is as follows: if a word or phrase occurs frequently in Mark it is regarded as characteristically Markan, and the presumption is that, whenever it occurs, Mark has introduced it; if a word or phrase occurs only occasionally in Mark it is regarded as uncharacteristic, and the presumption is that, whenever it occurs, it comes from the tradition. For example, Mark 8:1 begins thus: ἐν ἐκείναις ταῖς ἡμέραις πάλιν πολλοῦ ὄχλου ὄντος (in those days again when a large crowd had gathered). Schmidt argues that the word πάλιν (again), being a favourite word of Mark's, is an editorial addition, but the phrase ἐν ἐκείναις ταῖς ἡμέραις (in those days), being rare in Mark, came from the tradition.[9] This kind of argument raises a number of questions.

First, the presupposition behind this argument is that the introductions to the stories Mark received from the tradition were all in a fixed form, which Mark either took over word for word or deliberately altered. Thus, although Schmidt believes that the tradition behind Mark's gospel was mainly an oral tradition, he is able to treat it as though it were a written tradition and apply to it the techniques associated with the textual criticism of manuscripts. As we saw earlier, this is a presupposition that Schmidt consistently makes, though he has no objective evidence to support it.[10]

Second, how do we decide which words are characteristic? This question is raised in an acute form by Schmidt's discussion of Mark 6:1: καὶ ἐξῆλθεν ἐκεῖθεν καὶ ἔρχεται εἰς τὴν πατρίδα αὐτοῦ. (And Jesus departed from there and came to his own country). Schmidt comments that at first sight this verse seems to provide a good connection between the preceding story (the healing of Jairus' daughter) and the following story (Jesus' rejection at Nazareth). But then, as usual, he finds a difficulty. The word ἐκεῖθεν (from there) occurs only five times in Mark and is therefore not a characteristically Markan word. This suggests to Schmidt that Mark has reproduced it from his source, where, like all travelling introductions, it was devoid of context. When the word ἐκεῖθεν occurs in Matthew, on the other hand, it can be regarded as an editorial addition. For one thing, Matthew is in the habit of using such link-words, and for another, he uses the word ἐκεῖθεν 12 times to Mark's five.[11]

How often does a word need to be used in an author's work to be regarded as characteristic? If we allow for the difference in length between Matthew and Mark, the ratio of occurrences of ἐκεῖθεν is roughly 3:2. This does not seem a significant enough difference to justify Schmidt's treatment of the word as characteristic of Matthew and uncharacteristic of Mark.

Third, even a demonstrably favourite word may on occasion be traditional. It is true that Mark, like every other author, has some favourite words, the most obvious being εὐθύς (immediately). But why should the word εὐθύς not have formed part of the tradition from time to time? If we assume that Mark was so fond of this word that he introduced it ten times as frequently as it occurred in the tradition, how are we to determine which of its occurrences represent the 90 per cent of cases of Markan addition, and which represent the 10 per cent of cases of Markan preservation of the tradition? The bare fact of its being a favourite word does not help us to make this decision.

Fourth, the fact that Mark uses a phrase rarely, or only once, does not prove that he has taken it from tradition. In the case of the phrase ἐν ἐκείναις ταῖς ἡμέραις in those days in Mark 8:1, Schmidt notes that this phrase appears elsewhere in Mark only once (1:9), though it would have been appropriate in many other places. Anyone who wants to attribute this phrase, or the whole section to which it belongs, to Mark must, so Schmidt declares, answer an insoluble question – why does Mark use this expression here and not elsewhere, whereas Matthew uses it often? He implies that, because no answer can be given to this question, the possibility that Mark could have used this phrase on his own initiative may be discounted.[12]

Scholars who argue in this way are projecting their own method of writing onto another author. The essence of Schmidt's style of writing is consistency: he starts from clearly defined presuppositions and applies them consistently to all the passages he discusses. Yet even in Schmidt's writing there are inconsistencies. For example, the concept of 'beginning' occurs frequently in the book. To express this idea he uses various words such as *anfangen*, *einsetzen* and *beginnen*. Were his use of these words to be analysed, I imagine that some words would be found to occur more frequently than others. If anyone were to ask the question why, in a particular passage, a less favourite word is used, this would be an insoluble question. But it would not justify us in attributing different sections of Schmidt's book to an E (*einsetzen*) source or to a B (*beginnen*) source, nor, if one of Schmidt's less favourite words happened to be a favourite word of Wellhausen or Johannes Weiss, would we be justified in attributing Schmidt's use of it in a particular passage to the influence of that scholar. Why, then, should we use such methods to analyse an author such as Mark, who may have varied his introductory formulae for reasons that we do not know and have no solid grounds for guessing?

Schmidt's underlying assumption seems to be that Mark was a primitive and unsophisticated writer, who must have operated with a small and limited vocabulary of oft-repeated words, so that any word occurring less than ten times must be regarded as imposed upon him by his sources. Once we begin to question Schmidt's low estimate of Mark's ability, it is surprising how many of his ancillary arguments lose their credibility. If Mark was a creative author, he would be free to use a less familiar word whenever he wished, for stylistic reasons or because he felt it to be appropriate to the context.

Mark 6:6 is a case in point. It reads: καὶ περιῆγεν τὰς κώμας κύκλω διδάσκων (and he toured the surrounding villages teaching). Most scholars in Schmidt's day regarded this verse as an editorial addition by Mark. But Schmidt thinks it could have been attached to the preceding narrative in the tradition. One of his reasons for taking this possibility so seriously is that this is the only occurrence of περιάγειν in Mark and that κύκλῳ occurs only rarely. He sees the fact that these are not favourite words of the evangelist as support for the view that the whole phrase was taken from the tradition.[13]

This argument is introduced rather hesitantly: statistics about these words, we are told, are not very productive, but 'it may perhaps be mentioned' that περιάγειν occurs only once and κύκλῳ rarely. Nevertheless, whether hesitantly or not, the argument is presented and needs to be examined. It is interesting that the words περιάγειν and κύκλῳ both occur once only in the Pauline letters (1 Cor. 9:5; Rom. 15:19). So far as I know, no one has suggested that either of these words is not authentically Pauline because it occurs only once in his extant letters, and one wonders why such an argument should be used in the case of Mark. Vocabulary depends to a large extent on context. Neither Paul nor Mark makes frequent reference to circular tours, and therefore they do not often need to use the vocabulary relating to a circular tour. Schmidt's hesitation in presenting this argument is justified.

In saying this, I do not wish to dispute Schmidt's judgment that the *content* of Mark 6:6 is drawn from tradition. What seems to me to be questionable is his view that Mark, being basically only a copyist, took over the precise language of his sources as well as their content, and that only his favourite words should be attributed to Mark himself.

It is not only specific chronological phrases that Schmidt regards as uncharacteristic of Mark, but chronological terms in general. The statement in 11:12 that Jesus and his disciples returned to Jerusalem 'on the following day' is attributed to tradition on the grounds that 'it is not Mark's style to embellish his narrative with chronological notes.'[14] Similarly, Schmidt argues that the phrase 'on that day' (ἐν ἐκείνῃ τῇ ἡμέρᾳ) in 4:35, if it was in Matthew or Luke, would be regarded as a link-phrase of the evangelist, but in the case of Mark phrases such as 'on that day' and 'when it was evening' are not characteristic, so Mark must have taken them from the tradition.[15] This argument is circular. The chronological statements in Mark are dismissed one by one as uncharacteristic; but the hypothesis that Markan chronological statements are uncharacteristic is dependent on the fact that all such statements have been individually dismissed.

With regard to Luke, Schmidt's approach is different. He thinks of Luke as a stylist, not just a copyist, and thus as in control of his use of vocabulary in a way he does not believe Mark to have been. However, the question still arises as to how far Luke's choice of vocabulary indicates the origin of his material. In Luke 1:56 we read that Mary stayed with Elizabeth for three months and then returned home. Schmidt describes this as a transitional verse, which enables Luke to periodize the events. He deduces the Lukan character of the verse not only from its content, but also from the use of the verb ὑποστρέφειν (return) which occurs far more frequently in Luke's writings than in the rest of the New Testament.[16] On the other hand, in commenting on Luke 18:35: ἐγένετο δὲ ἐν τῷ ἐγγίζειν αὐτὸν εἰς Ἰερείχω (and it came to pass as he was drawing near to Jericho) Schmidt argues that, though the style is typically Lukan with its use of ἐγένετο , the content of the verse is taken from Mark.[17] Comparison of these two comments suggests that the use of characteristic words and expressions is not a reliable guide to the source of the information conveyed.

iii) The criterion of multiple context

According to the criterion of multiple context, whenever similar sayings or stories appear in the gospels in different contexts, only one of those contexts can be original. For example, Matthew's version of the healing of the man with the withered hand (12:9–14) includes the statement by Jesus that a sheep that has fallen into a pit on the sabbath will be rescued. Schmidt believes this saying to be drawn from the sayings-source 'Q', and asserts that Luke has placed the same saying at a different point in his gospel. He deduces from this that in Matthew the saying is not in its original context.[18] There are two assumptions lying behind this argument that need to be examined.

a) The term 'original context' (*ursprüngliche Stelle*) makes sense only on the assumption that Jesus never repeated himself – that he could not possibly have used the same argument in a synagogue (as described by Matthew) and in a Pharisee's house (as described by Luke). The only reason for this assumption is mere dogma. All preachers and teachers repeat themselves, especially peripatetic preachers, whose task is to proclaim the same message of the Kingdom of God in many different places. There is no reason to believe that Jesus was an exception to this rule.

Take, for example, the passages that refer to the two great commandments, to love God and love your neighbour. All three synoptic gospels record a conversation in which these two commandments are quoted. In Matthew and Mark the conversation occurs between the triumphal entry and the passion, when Jesus is asked by a scribe which is the greatest commandment, and cites the two commandments in reply. Luke records a conversation much earlier in Jesus's ministry: a scribe asks how he can gain eternal life, and when Jesus asks him what the scripture says, he cites the two commandments. Subsequently he asks the further question, 'Who is my neighbour?' and Jesus tells the parable of the good Samaritan (Matt. 22:34–40; Mark 12:28–34; Luke 10: 25–37).

Schmidt assumes that all three synoptic accounts are versions of a single conversation. In his opinion Luke has transferred the story to an earlier stage in the ministry of Jesus because such a friendly conversation between Jesus and a scribe would not fit his portrayal of the increasing hostility to Jesus after the triumphal entry.[19] But the Lukan account differs so greatly from the account in Matthew and Mark that there seems little reason, apart from pure dogma, to regard them as variant versions of the same story. Almost the only point of resemblance between the two accounts is the combination of the two commandments. The only possible ground for Schmidt's interpretation is the assumption that these two commandments could have been brought together only once in the ministry of Jesus. The absurdity of this assumption has been exposed by T.W. Manson, who argued that 'great teachers constantly repeat themselves':

> If a modern teacher of religion thought of such a thing as that, he would print it and it would make its way into the minds of the million. But in the first century A.D. in Palestine the only way of publishing great thoughts was to go on repeating them in talk or sermons.[20]

Schmidt's argument relies on what I have called elsewhere 'the law of non-repetition' – a law that runs contrary to both common sense and experience.[21] In the introduction to the *Oxford University Press Dictionary of Quotations* Bernard Darwin points out that Sherlock Holmes scholars, despite the high standards they set themselves, often find it difficult to recollect the original context of a quotation. This is particularly true of the remarks of Dr. Watson. He was so constantly saying that his practice was not very absorbing or that he had an accommodating neighbour that it is hard to remember when he said which.[22] Had Schmidt been a Sherlock Holmes scholar, he could have provided a very simple solution to this problem: Dr. Watson made these remarks on one occasion and in one context only, and the occurrence of similar remarks in other contexts must be due to the work of a later editor of the Holmes tradition.

b) The second assumption lying behind Schmidt's argument is that, where two sayings or stories share the same general content but differ in detail, they should be treated as variant versions of a single original. In the case of the animals rescued on the sabbath, the sayings in Matthew and Luke differ considerably. Matthew writes of a sheep falling into a pit; Luke writes of a son or an ox falling into a well. If this is indeed a 'Q' saying, as Schmidt believes, either Matthew or Luke has drastically altered it for no obvious reason.

The same is true of Luke's account of the Last Supper, which contains a lot of material absent from the parallel accounts in Matthew and Mark. Schmidt comments that, in the Lukan version, Jesus 'says various words of farewell to his disciples which are introduced either earlier or later by Mark and Matthew.'[23] What this comment ignores is that most of the teaching reported by Luke in 22:21–38 differs markedly from any possible parallels in Mark and Matthew. Schmidt's theory implies that each of these sayings has been deliberately altered by one or other evangelist – a view that does not square with his normal portrayal of the evangelists as unimaginative copyists, but is nevertheless a defensible position. The trouble is that Schmidt does not defend it but presumes it. His adherence to the criterion of multiple context leads him to believe, as a simple matter of deduction from first principles, that when a gospel saying has a parallel in another gospel, whether close or tenuous, all the variants must derive from a single original saying.

However, in this respect as in so many others Schmidt is not totally consistent. When commenting on the parallel passages Luke 7:29f. and Matt. 21:32, in which similar sentiments are expressed in almost totally different language, he says it is uncertain whether they both go back to the same tradition 'as is commonly assumed'.[24] Schmidt here reveals his independence of the assumptions of his contemporaries, but elsewhere seems bound by the same rigid thought-forms as they.

We can see the same ambivalence in Schmidt's approach to doublet theories, in which the criterion of multiple context is applied to a whole pericope or a whole section of a gospel. Sometimes he agrees with such theories. He regards it as certain that the stories of feeding the five thousand and the four thousand are doublets;[25] and Luke's account of Jesus's address to the 70(72) missioners is described as 'an unmistakable doublet of the address to the twelve apostles in Mk 6 and Mt 10'.[26] In one case he detects not a doublet but a triplet. The healing of the centurion's servant (Matt. 8:5–13; Luke 7:1–10), the healing of the royal official's son (John 4:46–54) and the healing of the daughter of the synagogue-leader Jairus (Mark 5:21–43 and parallels) are treated as variant forms of a single tradition. The difference between a centurion, a royal official and a synagogue-leader on the one hand, and the difference between a servant, a son and a daughter on the other hand, are described as 'small differences that emerged in the course of oral tradition'.[27]

In other cases, however, Schmidt is highly critical of doublet theories. Mark 6:14–16 describes various speculations about Jesus' identity that had come to the ears of Herod. Some scholars had argued that these verses were a doublet of 8:28 (the speculations reported to Jesus by his disciples at Caesarea Philippi). But Schmidt disagrees. He asserts that the Jewish people must have puzzled over who Jesus was again and again, and would go back again and again to the great figures of Moses and Elijah. Why then, he asks, should not both 6:14–16 and 8:28 be historical?[28] He is also critical of the view of Wrede and Wendling that the reference to a child in Mark 9:36f. is taken from Mark 10:13ff., and accuses them of overdependence on a theory of doublets.[29] He is even more scathing about the attempt of Wendling to see Mark 1:16–31 and Mark 4:35–5:34 as doublets. Both these passages describe an event related to the lake, an exorcism, some miracles and the healing of a woman. Wendling's attempt to deduce from this parallel sequence, despite all the differences in detail, that the two passages are doublets, is described by Schmidt as 'a prime example of affected sophistry' (*ein Musterbeispiel gesuchtester Spitzfindigkeit*).[30]

The question raised by all this is: what are the criteria for identifying doublets? The fact that similar incidents are described in similar ways does not make them automatically into the same incident. For example, in each of the triplet stories an official requests Jesus to come to his house to heal a member of his household; but it is precisely people in official positions who would be most likely to make such a request. To describe all the manifold variations between the three accounts as small differences that emerged in the course of oral tradition is to attribute to the supposed storytellers of the early church a degree of irresponsibility for which there is no evidence, and is difficult to reconcile with Schmidt's theory of the fixed wording of oral tradition.

It is true that, in Kenneth Bailey's experience of informal controlled oral tradition, 'the story teller had a certain freedom to tell the story in his own way as long as the central thrust of the story was not changed'.[31] But Schmidt has turned this idea on its head. The items he regards as freely changeable, such as the identity of the main characters, are precisely the items which, if we follow Bailey's model, cannot be changed. The items he regards as fixed and immovable are the introductory formulae, such as 'after some days', that are not essential to the story.

Throughout his book Schmidt seems to work with two mutually inconsistent models. According to Model A, oral tradition consisted of fixed stories with a fixed wording that Mark took over as they stood, inserting a favourite word or explanatory phrase here and there in order to create a connected narrative. According to Model B, oral tradition felt free to alter synagogue-leaders into royal officials or vice versa as it pleased. Since Schmidt's theory of early church storytellers has, on his own admission, no objective evidence to support it, they can as easily be credited with one method of working as another. It is difficult to believe, however, that even imaginary people could have conformed to two contradictory models at the same time.

iv) Conclusion

The main problem with Schmidt's approach to literary criticism is that he takes no account of the way books are actually written. When employing the argument from silence, for example, he does not consider the pressures that force authors to leave out items they would like to include; he simply attributes Mark's omissions to his ignorance or to the scantiness of his sources. When employing the argument from contradiction, he does not consider the possibility that variation in vocabulary could be a stylistic feature, or allow for the deliberate use of paradox, whether by Jesus or by the evangelists; every word must have a consistent and uniform meaning, as in a scientific textbook. Literary criticism means for Schmidt the mechanical application of criteria relating to vocabulary and style rather than the attempt to understand the evangelists as creative authors. He seeks to bring works of art under the rule of law.

It would be an interesting exercise to apply Schmidt's criteria to Aylward Shorter's book *Priest in the Village*.[32] This book is a record of the author's experiences while living in a village called Mazimbo belonging to a Tanzanian tribe called the Kimbu. In his preface he writes:

> Everything in this book really happened. My Kimbu friends who come across it will notice a necessary foreshortening and simplification of some incidents. I have had to leave out many names of persons and places in order to make for easier reading. For the same reason I have translated vernacular terms wherever possible and have not followed a strict chronological order in the narrative. It has been necessary to group experiences and events under certain headings. In writing this book, I have relived my life in Mazimbo with a certain amount of intensity. I have consulted my diaries and notes, listened to tape recordings, scrutinized maps and photographs, and even revisited the area in person. Above all, I have prayed over this book, and many things have become clearer to me in the praying and in the writing.[33]

Shorter admits to many of the 'defects' that Schmidt points out in the gospels – foreshortening and simplification of incidents, omission of names of people and places, lack of strict chronological order and topical grouping of incidents. He also confesses to a design: the book expresses convictions that have crystallized in his mind through prayer and meditation. But all these 'defects' (except for the 'defect' of design) are of literary origin – their purpose is to make the book easier to read. They do not alter the fact that the whole book is based on eyewitness evidence and that it 'really happened'. Even the fact that the book has a design does not prove that Shorter has distorted the facts in the interests of periodizing and psychologizing (to quote Schmidt's favourite charge against Luke).

Accordingly, when we do read definite statements of time and place in Shorter's book, we do not follow Schmidt's methodology and discount them on the grounds that such statements are absent elsewhere. We read on page 190: 'The second time I made the pilgrimage to Nsansaa was in December at the beginning of the rainy season.' If we employed Schmidt's methods, we should have to cast doubt on virtually the whole of this statement. We should deduce from what we had learnt of Shorter's literary technique in other passages that he must have followed the same procedure in this one. If we did this, we should be falling into the same trap as Schmidt – the temptation to apply to the work of a human author the kind of rigid criteria that properly apply to the world of machines.[34]

Notes

1   *Rahmen* 16f.: 'Even scholars such as J. Weiss and Wellhausen, who have said a lot that is correct about Mark's characteristics, are still too much under the spell of the traditional evaluation, that is to say the overvaluation of Mark as a good historical source. . . . Spitta has correctly shown that in many cases Luke and even John provide better historical information. But Spitta was led by historical considerations to the unquestioning formulation of a literary judgment that cannot be sustained. In general the historical and literary approaches are intertwined far too much in scholarly research. Advocates of the Markan hypothesis have the correct literary appreciation that Mark is the earliest gospel, but draw from this fact the false historical conclusion that it has on the whole more historical worth than the other gospels. . . . It is illegitimate to proceed automatically from recognition of the historical worthlessness of the Markan outline to endorsement of the Johannine outline, or to find in John the clues to the correct approach to Mark. It is far better to elucidate on its own terms the earliest framework of the ministry of Jesus as contained in the second gospel. This can only be done by detailed literary critical investigations, with particular consideration of the synoptic question and of textual criticism.'

2   Ibid. 78. This is Schmidt's preferred translation. An alternative translation takes the words δι' ἡμερῶν with ἠκούσθη : 'and he entered Capernaum again and after some time news got around that he was in the house.' The difference in translation does not affect Schmidt's argument.

3   Ibid. 79.

4   Ibid. 283f.: 'As a preliminary to our evaluation of the connection of events in Mark one fact can be seen to be significant: Mark's account of the temple cleansing, which seems at first sight to have been so excellently built in between the fig-tree episodes and their chronological data, was removed from its place at the earliest possible stage without any damage to the context.'

5   Ibid. 291–3.

6   Ibid. 218.

7   Ibid. 50.

8   Ibid. 245 n. 1.

9   Ibid. 192.

10 See Chapter 1 section ii) on the theory of travelling introductions.

11 *Rahmen* 153.

12 Ibid. 192.

13 Ibid. 159.

14 Ibid. 300.

15 Ibid. 135.

16 Ibid. 312.

17 Ibid. 264.

18 Ibid. 102. The Lukan parallel is Luke 14:5.

19 Ibid. 281–2.

20 T.W. Manson, *The Sayings of Jesus* (SCM Press, London 1949) 260.

21 Hall, *Seven Pillories* 87–90.

22 Bernard Darwin, *The Oxford University Press Dictionary of Quotations*, (Chancellor Press, London 1985[2]) xvii.

23 *Rahmen* 306

24 Ibid. 118.

25 Ibid. 192.

26 Ibid. 168.

27 Ibid. 73f.

28 Ibid. 174.

29 Ibid. 231 n. 2.

30 Ibid. 151 n. 1. Compare also Schmidt's refusal (p. 119) to regard the anointing story in Luke 7:36–50 as a doublet of the anointing stories in the other gospels on account of the great differences between them.

31 Bailey, *Oral Tradition* (Themelios edition) 7.

32 Aylward Shorter, *Priest in the Village* (Cassell, London 1979).

33 Ibid. vi f.

34 For a more general discussion of the mechanization of literary criticism in New Testament study see *Seven Pillories* chapter 2: 'The Argument from Probable Certainty' pp. 21–36.

Part II

7

Mark 1:4–8 (*Rahmen* 18–24)

Mark 1:4–8 states that John the Baptist preached in the wilderness and baptized in the Jordan. Schmidt's aim is to show that these two statements are mutually inconsistent and have different origins: that the Jordan location came from Mark's source, but the wilderness location was a Markan addition.

He begins with the *argument from contradiction*. Mark records that John preached in the wilderness, that people from Jerusalem and the whole of Judaea went out to hear him, and that he baptized them in the Jordan. The text of verse 4 is uncertain, some manuscripts reading that 'John baptized and preached in the wilderness', others that 'John the Baptizer preached in the wilderness'. Schmidt prefers the latter reading (which does not specifically say that John baptized in the wilderness) but nevertheless believes the clear implication of Mark's narrative to be that the place of baptizing was identical with the place of preaching – in other words, that the river Jordan was in the wilderness. This creates for Schmidt a difficulty that cannot be resolved by defining the wilderness (ἔρημος) as the lower Jordan valley (described by Josephus in one place as ἐρημία); we should rather think of a genuine wilderness of sand or rock, such as is suggested by the description of John's lifestyle in verse 6. A further problem is that according to verse 12 Jesus went into the wilderness after his baptism; but in Schmidt's view Mark's narrative implies that Jesus was already in the wilderness at the time of his baptism. So there are geographical discrepancies (*lokale Unstimmigkeiten*).

In this discussion, as is often the case in Schmidt's book, the *argument from contradiction* is closely linked with the *argument from silence*. His argument seems to run as follows: i) Mark states that John preached in the wilderness and does not specifically mention that he ever left the wilderness. ii) This must mean that, in Mark's opinion, he never did leave the wilderness. iii) Therefore, if he baptized in the Jordan, Mark must locate the Jordan in the wilderness. It is true that Schmidt's interpretation is not absolutely literal. If the wilderness consisted either of sand or of rock, and if John literally baptized in the wilderness, then he must have baptized either with sand or with stone. This would create an inconsistency with verse 8, which refers to baptism with water. However, Schmidt does not mention this inconsistency. Though he has a low opinion of Mark's intelligence, there are limits to the degree of stupidity he is willing to attribute to him.

Another factor is the contrast between the brief statement of the location of John's ministry in Mark and Matthew and the more detailed comments in the other two gospels. According to the fourth gospel, John baptized at various places on both sides of the Jordan (1:28; 3:23; 10:40). According to Luke (3:2f.), the word of the Lord came to John in the wilderness, and he then went into the whole area around the Jordan (εἰς πᾶσαν τὴν περίχωρον τοῦ Ἰορδάνου). The Lukan picture of an initial call in the wilderness followed by a peripatetic ministry over a wide area makes good sense, and is only inconsistent with Mark if one relies on the *argument from silence* in the way Schmidt does, and regards Mark's concise summary as a complete statement of John's movements.

At this point Schmidt makes an interesting comment. He sees it as illegitimate to understand Mark and Matthew in the light of Luke. Mark and Matthew, he argues, offer the more difficult and therefore the more original reading: if anyone believes the wilderness scenery to be historical, he may regard Luke's presentation also as historical; but this does not alter the fact that Mark's is the older account. Above all, Schmidt rejects the 'harmonization' of the Catholic exegetes such as Pölzl, who believed that John began his ministry in the wilderness and then moved to the Jordan. 'These efforts at harmonization demonstrate clearly the inconsistency of the text.'

The question raised by Schmidt's approach is this: should one apply the techniques of textual criticism and talk of earlier and later readings when discussing the composition of the gospels? Schmidt quotes the judgment of J. Weiss that Luke's presentation is here more convincing than Mark's and asks, 'Does he mean by this that Luke's is the older narrative?' The implication of this question is that no gospel narrative can be historical unless it is chronologically the oldest. Schmidt pours scorn on Luke's presentation not because it is implausible but because he believes it to byhntgbm,.e later, in accordance with the principle, 'the earlier, the purer'[1]. This is, of course, consistent with his presupposition that Luke never has any additional sources of information apart from his primary source (in this case Mark). By virtue of this presupposition any attempt to regard the gospel accounts of a particular event as complementary rather than contradictory can be rejected on principle as harmonization. Any item mentioned in the 'secondary' account and not mentioned in the 'primary' account is *ipso facto* to be dismissed as historically worthless.

Schmidt then proceeds to analyse the reasons for Mark's supposed contradictions. He appeals first to the *theory of Markan artlessness*. Mark, he asserts, had no clear idea of the geography of Palestine and no interest in the matter. That is why he describes Jesus as going into the wilderness after having been baptized in the wilderness. Schmidt seems to assume that this is the sort of discrepancy an artless author such as Mark could easily overlook. As to the motive for Mark's procedure, this can be deduced with the help of the *argument from design*. Mark has just quoted the reference in Isaiah 40 to 'a voice crying in the wilderness'. He has therefore introduced the wilderness motif into John's ministry to fit in with the Isaiah quotation. In so doing he was not thinking of any particular wilderness, but 'a magnificent picture of desolate solitude floated before his mind' (*ihm schwebte ein grandioses Bild der wüsten Einsamkeit vor*). As is usual with the *argument from design*, the more vivid the critic's imagination, the more strikingly can Mark's imagination be reconstructed.

In Schmidt's opinion Mark invented not only John's wilderness preaching but also the supporting details in verse 6 about his clothing of camel's hair, his leather girdle and his diet of locusts and wild honey. Allegations of this sort are impossible to prove or disprove. Schmidt cannot produce any evidence to establish his reconstruction of Mark's procedure, and equally there is no evidence to refute it. But the portrait of Mark that Schmidt paints does seem a little inconsistent. On the one hand he regards Mark as 'on the whole only a compiler', who took over the stories of Jesus from early church storytellers along with the meaningless introductory formulae that accompanied them, and was too conservative to alter anything. On the other hand Mark is said to have invented John's wilderness ministry, and all the vivid details of clothing and diet that went with it, on the basis of a single word in an Old Testament quotation.

Since Schmidt's picture of Mark is based on imagination rather than on evidence, he is free to construct a Mark who is full of contradictions if he so wishes. But there is no reason why subsequent scholarship should take such a construction seriously.

The view that John's wilderness preaching is a Markan invention is then confirmed by two other arguments. First comes an *argument from silence*. There is no mention of the wilderness in the Ebionite gospel or in the fourth gospel. The former source he describes as 'a parallel fragment from the Ebionite gospel as handed down by Epiphanius'. After beginning with a precise time-statement the fragment continues: 'A man called John came, baptizing in the river Jordan with a baptism of repentance. He was said to be a descendant of Aaron the priest and the son of Zachariah and Elisabeth.' I do not see how we can read any significance whatsoever into the omissions of such a brief fragmentary statement as this. In the case of the fourth gospel, its omissions cover a lot more than the wilderness. There is, for instance, no mention in the fourth gospel of John's message of repentance, an item that is included in the Ebionite fragment. The account of John the Baptist in the fourth gospel is so selective, and concentrates so exclusively on John's testimony to Jesus as Messiah, that its omission of other matters is clearly content-oriented. Thus neither of the two silences has any evidential value for assessing the accuracy of Mark's narrative. Nevertheless, by referring to them Schmidt manages to create an atmosphere of doubt and a general impression of Mark's unreliability.

There then follows an appeal to the *criterion of detachability*. Schmidt points out that the references to the wilderness in verse 4 and to John's wilderness lifestyle in verse 6 can be omitted without damaging the smooth flow of the narrative. Those who believe the *criterion of detachability* to be a logically valid criterion will no doubt be impressed by this argument. Those who accept Schmidt's own admission of the criterion's fallibility will be less impressed.

When we survey all these arguments, it is clear that none of them proves the point Schmidt is trying to make. His argument is cumulative in the sense that, by accumulating a whole series of unsound arguments, he creates a general atmosphere of uncertainty. When this accumulation of arguments is read through quickly it seems quite impressive. It is only when each argument is examined in detail that one realizes how weak his case is. His conclusions are valid only if we make the following assumptions:

a)   Mark's failure to mention any movement by John from his original location must mean that in Mark's opinion he never did move, but exercised the whole of his ministry in the place where he started.

b)   Mark was happy to invent locations for his stories and supporting details for those locations whenever it suited his design.

c)   Mark was too stupid to notice the contradictions in his narrative resulting from these additions.

d)   No statement in Luke that is not found in the parallel passage in Mark has any value as historical evidence, because in those passages where Mark is his primary source Luke never has any source of information apart from Mark.

e)   Any statement that is made by one or more of our sources but omitted by another must be treated as historically dubious, no matter how fragmentary or theologically slanted the omitting source may be.

f)   All statements that can be smoothly detached from their context (i.e. the bulk of the gospel narrative) must be treated with suspicion for that reason.

Note

1   For a more general discussion of this maxim, see *Seven Pillories* 28–30.

8

Mark 1:14f. and parallels
(*Rahmen* 32–38)

Mark 1:14f. states that 'after the arrest of John [the Baptist] Jesus came to Galilee'. Schmidt's aim is to show that this statement is pure invention and that Mark has no knowledge of either the chronology or the topography involved.

He begins with the *argument from silence* and produces a catalogue of Mark's deficiencies. Mark's statement seems to him to be very imprecise. When, he asks, was John arrested? How much time elapsed between the temptation of Jesus (which immediately precedes these verses in Mark) and John's imprisonment? What was the motivation for Jesus coming to Galilee? Under what circumstances did John disappear from the scene? Did Jesus come directly from the wilderness to Galilee? What exactly is meant by the term 'Galilee'? Since Mark does not provide the answer to any of these questions, Schmidt's conclusion is clear: verses 14 and 15 are a generalizing summary, composed by Mark to provide a bridge between the temptation story and the Galilee stories that follow. His reason for writing it is not knowledge of the facts but his desire to schematize the ministry of Jesus: Jesus must be seen to work not in parallel with John but after him – the old must pass away before the new can come.

In order to evaluate this example of the *argument from silence* let us imagine how these two verses would need to be expanded if all the items Schmidt regards as essential were included:

'In the eighth month of the sixteenth year of Tiberius Caesar John the Baptist was arrested by Herod. There were two main reasons for this: the increasing following John had gained with its implicit threat to political stability, and the fact that John had criticized Herod's marriage to his sister-in-law. After his temptations, Jesus had been preaching for three and a half months not far from John near the lower Jordan river, but when he heard of John's imprisonment he decided it was wise to move north to Galilee, a move he had always intended to make when the time was right. He took the route west of the Jordan valley, passed through Samaria, began preaching in the Gennesaret area and then moved through Galilee steadily northwards.'

If Mark had written in this style, he would have produced a gospel ten times as long and very different in character. Mark was not writing a scholarly academic work, but a book designed to appeal to ordinary people. The only way to make a story-line flow freely is to omit unnecessary details. But Schmidt seems unaware of such literary factors. He assumes that Mark must have reproduced all the information available to him, and that his failure to mention things that we in the twentieth century would like to know must in every case be due to the deficiencies of his sources.

Schmidt's second weapon is the *argument from literary criticism*. The style of these two verses is that of a generalizing summary (*Sammelbericht*); they are not written in the epic narrative style of most Markan pericopes, and therefore in Schmidt's opinion should be attributed to Mark himself. The implication is not only that Mark composed these verses (which would be generally accepted) but also that he did so out of his own head with no tradition to draw on. In evaluating this argument we must distinguish between fact and interpretation.

The fact of a difference in style is not in dispute. There are bound to be differences in style between miracle stories and generalizing summaries. A narrative will have a narrative style, a summary will have a summarizing style. This is equally true whether the material is Markan or traditional. Schmidt's judgment here is not really based on style but on his presupposition that Mark's sources were totally uninterested in the historical background of the stories they told. If this presupposition is true, the stories in Mark's sources cannot have contained any general statements, and must inevitably have lacked the style and vocabulary associated with general statements. Therefore, any passage exhibiting such style and vocabulary must automatically be labelled a Markan addition. Schmidt's argument, which purports to be an argument about style, is in fact an *argument from presuppositions*.

The main argument in this section, however, is the *argument from design*. Schmidt's aim is to show that all four gospels are presenting not historical fact but their own point of view. This discussion is thus a good indicator as to how far the *argument from design* is a valid argument.

The core of Schmidt's argument is the contrast between Mark and the fourth gospel. Mark begins his gospel with a summary of the ministry of John the Baptist (1:1–8), and a brief description of the baptism and temptation of Jesus (1:9–13). This is immediately followed by the statement in verse 14 that after John's imprisonment Jesus came to Galilee. There is thus no record in Mark of Jesus and John exercising parallel ministries near the Jordan such as we find in the fourth gospel. Mark does not say that Jesus came *directly* from the temptations to Galilee, and therefore Schmidt correctly observes that there is no contradiction between the two gospels. But he hastens to add that in making this observation he is not concerned with harmonization or with seeking to rescue the fourth gospel as a historical source. His methodology with regard to any gospel is to take as his starting-point the author's intention. In his opinion the aim of the author of the fourth gospel was to score a point in his polemic against the disciples of John the Baptist, by showing that John was not the only one to baptize – Jesus also baptized at the same time. Mark, on the other hand, was following a '*Schema*', a pattern of salvation history, which required the old (John the Baptist) to pass away before the new (Jesus) could come. Thus both gospel writers are schematic, and their statements cannot be trusted.

The problem with this is that it proves too much. Either Jesus and John did exercise parallel ministries or they did not. If they did, then the fourth gospel, despite its tendentiousness, has recorded a historical fact. If they did not, then Mark, despite his schematism, was right to omit any reference to such a ministry. So Schmidt ends up sitting on the fence: 'The possibility remains that Jesus did work alongside John the Baptist. So it is an open question whether in 1:14f. Mark was reporting the real beginning of his public ministry or not.' This discussion reveals the barrenness of the *argument from design*. The motives Schmidt attributes to the two evangelists may or may not be correct. We can only conjecture the circumstances under which the fourth gospel was written; and modern attempts to find a logical pattern in Mark may be more indicative of the critic's determination to schematize Mark than of Mark's determination to schematize his material. But even if the fourth gospel's reference to parallel ministries and Mark's omission of such a reference are both dogmatically motivated, they cannot both be historically incorrect. The canon 'if schematic, then unhistorical' cannot be true in both cases; so why should it be true in either?

Again, we may test Schmidt's methodology by applying it to a modern situation. Let us suppose that there is a general election, and I receive election literature from several parties. The Government party proclaims positive achievements in fields such as health and education. The other parties point out deficiencies in the health and education services. When reading this literature I recognize that all the authors are highly motivated and therefore selective in the facts they record. But I do not automatically assume that those facts are inaccurate. I realize that it is in the political interests of the various authors to be accurate, since some of the readers will have first-hand knowledge of the areas under discussion. Therefore I harmonize. I seek to arrive at a balanced judgment that holds together both the positive achievements and the deficiencies in the fields under review.

Harmonization is a normal and logical response of a floating voter to political leaflets that present mutually contradictory points of view. Why, then, should harmonization be regarded as illegitimate in the case of the much less strident differences between Mark and John? Both Mark and John were evangelists, seeking to promote a specific point of view. Mark's aim was to present 'the good news of Jesus Christ the Messiah' (1:1). John's aim was to help his readers to believe that Jesus was the Christ, the Son of God (20:31). Like modern pamphleteers they knew that at least some of their readers would have expert knowledge, either because they were eyewitnesses themselves or because they had heard the stories of Jesus from the lips of eyewitnesses. Even if we assume, with Schmidt, that Mark was unable or unwilling to make contact with any eyewitnesses himself, he could not have imposed a similar limitation on his readers. Therefore accuracy would be as much in their interests as in those of a modern political activist. There is no logical correlation between the commitment of an author to a faith or ideology and the accuracy of that author's statements. Inaccuracy needs to be established by evidence, not assumed on principle.

Schmidt then turns to Matthew's statement (4:12) that Jesus went away (ἀνεχώρησεν) to Galilee after hearing that John had been arrested. He takes the verb to mean that Jesus withdrew or retreated to Galilee to get away from Herod, and points out that Galilee was also under Herod's jurisdiction. In Schmidt's opinion Matthew has overlooked this because he did not have any true idea of the historical details and did not bother much about such things.

This argument, like so many of Schmidt's arguments, sounds impressive until you start to question the underlying assumption. The verb ἀναχωρέω is used by Matthew in two senses: i) to return – e.g. the wise men returned home (2:12); ii) to depart – e.g. Jesus tells the mourners to depart from Jairus' house (9:24) and Judas, after returning the thirty pieces of silver, went away and hanged himself (27:5). In some cases the departure is a tactical withdrawal – e.g. Joseph's departure to Egypt (2:14) or Jesus leaving a place where they were plotting to kill him (12:15). Such a connotation derives from the context and is not inherent in the verb. It may well be appropriate in the case of Jesus's departure to Galilee in 4:12. But if so, it would be perfectly reasonable for Jesus to move from an area where he was known to be an associate of John the Baptist to one where he was not so known, or to move from foreign territory to home territory. This would only be unreasonable if John's arrest were part of a deliberate policy of religious persecution throughout Herod's domain – a theory for which there is no evidence, and which runs contrary to Matthew's later statement (14:3f.) that the reason for John's arrest was his opposition to Herod's marriage.

Schmidt then applies the *argument from design* to Matthew. Matthew states that Jesus, after leaving Nazareth, went to live in Capernaum in the territory of Zebulun and Naphtali. He then quotes some verses from Isaiah that refer to Galilee, and to the territory of Zebulun and Naphtali, as a place where people sitting in darkness see a great light. In Schmidt's opinion these verses (Matt. 4:12–17) give us a clear insight into the way Matthew set about his work. So he reconstructs Matthew's procedure as follows: the only historical information available to Matthew was the statement in Mark that Jesus began his ministry in Galilee. Matthew wanted to support this with a word of scripture and the Isaiah quotation suited his purpose. He knew that Capernaum lay within the territory of Zebulun and Naphtali and therefore portrayed Jesus as going to live in Capernaum. But, since Jesus belonged to Nazareth, it would not have been right for him to go straight to Capernaum and avoid his home town, so Nazareth was introduced in a subordinate clause. Schmidt concludes that, when the text is analysed in this manner, the question as to whether Matthew has preserved any good historical tradition in point of detail is a question one no longer dares to ask.

Schmidt here employs the aetiological argument (a subspecies of the *argument from design*), according to which any narrative illustrated by a quotation from the Old Testament must be presumed to be a product of the quotation. In the present case this argument proves too much. The territory of Zebulun and Naphtali covered roughly the same area as the province of Galilee in Roman times. Therefore, if the aetiological argument is sound, it must be Matthew's reference to Galilee that is derived from the Old Testament reference to Zebulun and Naphtali. But this creates a problem for Schmidt. Matthew, he believes, was using Mark as his source, and the fact that Jesus went to Galilee is clearly stated in Mark. He therefore discerns the aetiological factor as residing, not in the mention of Galilee, but in the mention of Capernaum.

This reconstruction raises several questions: i) How could Matthew be aware that Capernaum lay within the territory of Zebulun and Naphtali if he was as ignorant of geography as Schmidt normally assumes him to have been? ii) Was Matthew aware that Nazareth and other Galilean towns were also in the same territory or did his geographical knowledge extend only to Capernaum? iii) Why should Matthew not have taken the Capernaum location also from Mark, since in Mark's account of the Galilee ministry Capernaum is the first town to be named (1:21)? Such questions either do not occur to Schmidt or do not bother him. His adherence to the *argument from design* requires him to derive Matthew's account from the Isaiah quotation; and since the only element in Matthew's account that can be so derived is the mention of Capernaum, this must be identified as the aetiological element, regardless of how plausible or implausible such a reconstruction may be.

According to Schmidt this passage provides a clear insight into the way Matthew worked. But what actually emerges from the discussion is a clear insight into the way Schmidt works. He proceeds by logical deduction from first principles. These principles require him to assume that Matthew was aware that Capernaum lay within the territory of Zebulun and Naphtali and, by implication, that he was unaware that other Galilean towns were also part of that territory. These assumptions are then presented as facts and the aetiological argument is put forward as though it were a deduction from evidence rather than (as in fact it is) a deduction from dogma.

Schmidt then turns his attention to Luke. The parallel passage in Luke (4:14f.) states that Jesus returned to Galilee in the power of the

Spirit, that his fame spread throughout the surrounding area and that he taught in their synagogues and was praised by everyone. Luke's account is so different from Mark's that many scholars in Schmidt's day believed it to be independent. But such a view would conflict with Schmidt's belief that, whenever there is a parallel in Mark, Mark is Luke's only source. He therefore sets out to show that each of the differences between Luke and Mark is due to Luke's deliberate alteration.

He reconstructs Luke's procedure as follows. Luke omits the reference to John's imprisonment because he has completed his account of John in 3:19f.; he omits the statement in Mark 1:14 that the content of Jesus's preaching was the kingdom of God because this may have seemed too narrow a description of that preaching, which included other things as well; he then adds a characteristically Lukan reference to the Spirit and a generalizing summary of the success of Jesus's mission, the details of which are drawn from the following chapters.

There are many analyses of this kind in Schmidt's book and they are all equally subjective. Schmidt's understanding of Luke's motives is conjectural, and another scholar could just as easily attribute different motives. For example, he argues that Luke omitted the Markan reference to Jesus preaching the kingdom of God because he thought this too narrow a description of Jesus' preaching. Yet a little later in the same chapter we find an exactly opposite situation, where according to Luke (4:43) Jesus says he was sent to preach the kingdom of God, whereas the Markan parallel (1:38) simply says 'preach'. The recurring question as to why one evangelist omits words and phrases that another evangelist includes is in most cases insoluble. Schmidt has as much right as anyone else to make an intelligent guess; but he does not have the right to use such guesses as evidence for Luke's editorial policy, especially in a case such as this where his attempt to read Luke's mind runs contrary to Luke's practice elsewhere.[1]

Nor is it legitimate to use the *argument from design* to establish the source (or lack of source) of Luke's information. Schmidt correctly describes the references to the Spirit and to the 'whole surrounding area' as characteristically Lukan. Luke elsewhere attributes movement from one place to another to the influence of the Spirit, and he often uses phrases such as 'the whole of Judaea, Galilee and Samaria' (Acts 9:31) or 'the whole of Joppa' (Acts 9:42). But this does not prove the point Schmidt is trying to establish – that in this passage Luke had no source of information apart from Mark. Luke was a stylist and a theologian. As a stylist he wrote in a characteristically Lukan style regardless of the source of his information. As a theologian he based his theology on interpretation of the available data, not simply on invention. The presence in a particular passage of Lukan style or Lukan theology tells us nothing whatsoever about the source (or lack of source) of the information given.

Conclusion

When we examine Schmidt's treatment of the four evangelists, we can see a common thread. In each case the historical statements they make are alleged to fit in with their motives and design, and this is taken to mean that they have invented these statements. There is a certain circularity in this argument. The motives attributed to the evangelists are conjectured from their narratives. Having conjectured these motives, Schmidt then accuses the evangelists of tendentiousness for making their narratives conform to them. The whole procedure leaves ample scope for scholarly imagination.

Note

1.   The text of Mark 1.14 is uncertain, and there may in fact not have been a reference to the kingdom of God in Mark's original manuscript. However, my main concern is not with the soundness or otherwise of Schmidt's judgment as a textual critic, but with the soundness or otherwise of the deductions he makes from the readings he adopts.

9

Luke 4:16–30 (*Rahmen* 38–43)

In this passage Luke describes the visit of Jesus to the synagogue in Nazareth, his teaching there and the hostility this teaching inspired. Schmidt's attack on Luke's accuracy may be divided into two sections, concerned respectively with chronology and topography.

a) Chronology

Schmidt begins with the *argument from contradiction*. He assumes that Luke made this the opening story in his account of the Galilee ministry because he believed it to be chronologically the first event in that ministry. In this respect Luke is seen to be inconsistent with Mark and Matthew, who locate Jesus' rejection at Nazareth towards the end of the Galilee ministry. Schmidt regards this as a deliberate alteration by Luke of his Markan source. He asks the question: 'How and why has Luke altered Mark's account which seemed to him unsatisfactory?' He finds the answer to this question in the *argument from design;* Luke wished to portray the Galilee ministry in stages, as a development from small to great in ever increasing circles, and also wished to explain why Jesus chose Capernaum as his base rather than Nazareth. In Schmidt's words, Luke was concerned to periodize the story of Jesus and present it biographically.

Schmidt also detects two internal contradictions in Luke's narrative. In verse 23 Jesus refers to previous miracles performed in Capernaum. This would be an impossibility if Jesus' visit to Nazareth came at the very beginning of his ministry. According to Schmidt this was agreed by most scholars of his day to be a contradiction – in Spitta's words a blatant discrepancy (*eine schreiende Unstimmigkeit*). He rejects the view that Luke realized there was a discrepancy in his source but was too conservative to remove it; rather, we should see here an example of Luke's incompetence. Luke, he writes, apparently overlooked this contradiction.

Presumably he would attribute the other alleged discrepancy to the same cause. According to verse 16 Jesus went into the synagogue *as his custom was*. Schmidt argues that this statement refers not only to Jesus' childhood habit of attending the synagogue but also to his adult habit of teaching in the synagogue, and is therefore inconsistent with Luke's belief that the Nazareth visit was Jesus' first visit to a synagogue since arriving in Galilee.

What should we make of these alleged contradictions? They all depend on the assumption that Luke believed Jesus' rejection at Nazareth to be chronologically the first event in the Galilee ministry. But Luke's words neither say this nor imply it. Luke 4:14–16 reads as follows: 'Jesus returned to Galilee in the power of the Spirit, and news of him spread through the whole surrounding area. He was teaching in their synagogues, glorified by all. And he came to Nazareth. . . .' Luke could not have stated more clearly that the visit to Nazareth took place at an unspecified point in an extensive preaching tour throughout Galilee. The periodizing motive that Schmidt attributes to Luke has no basis in the text. The contradiction is not with Luke's text but with Schmidt's reconstruction.

Why is Schmidt so convinced that, in Luke's understanding, this was Jesus's first visit to a synagogue since arriving in Galilee? Presumably he is relying on the *argument from silence*. Since Luke has not mentioned a specific synagogue visit before 4:16, he cannot have believed that there was one. The argument from silence is suspect at all times. In a case such as this, when Luke has referred in the previous verse to Jesus teaching throughout the synagogues of Galilee, it becomes ridiculous. Luke's allusions to Jesus' custom of synagogue attendance and to his previous miracles at Capernaum are not a sign of Luke's stupidity in failing to recognize a blatant contradiction. They are a reference back to the overall context given in verses 14f., and an indication to his readers that the story of the rejection at Nazareth is placed early in his gospel for programmatic rather than chronological reasons.

Schmidt's final argument about chronology is an *argument from textual tradition*. Marcion transferred this passage to a later point in the chapter, between verses 39 and 40. The probable reason for this transposition, as Schmidt rightly says, is the reference in verse 23 to

earlier miracles in Capernaum and Marcion's feeling that there should
be some account of Jesus's activity in Capernaum preceding this
reference. Schmidt concedes that Marcion's location is unsatisfactory
and cannot be original. But he nevertheless devotes half a page to
expounding the significance of Marcion's procedure for our understanding of how the gospels were composed. Marcion was able to lift
this passage without altering its framework and place it in a new
location. According to Schmidt this was precisely the way in which
Matthew and Luke treated Mark, and in which Mark treated the oral
tradition.

There are two curious features about this argument. One we have
discussed earlier – the idea that written sources and oral tradition were
so similar to each other that they could be handled by their editors in
an identical way. The other is even more curious – the way in which
Matthew, Mark, Luke and Marcion are regarded not as individuals
but as specimens of a type: what one does they all do. Suppose I were
to write in such terms about more recent authors, suggesting for
example that Bultmann and Dibelius had followed a certain procedure and therefore Schmidt must have followed the same procedure
because German scholars are much of a muchness. Such remarks, I
imagine, would be deemed unacceptable. Why, then, should similar
remarks about early Christian authors be deemed acceptable? Luke,
we are told, must have behaved in a certain manner, not because the
evidence shows that he did, but because a second-century heretic
behaved in this manner and early Christians were all the same. The
assumption seems to be that early Christian authors were primitive
people, who could all be expected to exhibit the same common
features of primitive society.

b) Topography

Schmidt's aim in discussing the topography of this passage is to show
that the events and sayings here recorded need not have any connection with Nazareth, but would fit another location equally well. There
are two sayings that seem to indicate a Nazareth location: the question
in verse 22, 'Is this not Joseph's son?' and the word in verse 24 about
prophets not being accepted in their home area. In both cases Schmidt
employs the *criterion of multiple context* and argues that these sayings
do not belong here because Mark records them in another context

(*an anderer Stelle*). When we look up this 'other context', it turns out to be the account of Jesus's rejection at Nazareth in Mark 6.

Let us look at this argument more closely. Schmidt believes that, for most of this passage, Luke is using a special tradition. But verse 22b and verse 24 are taken from Mark and must therefore be deleted as foreign to their Lukan context. The fact that the passage concerned in Mark refers to the same situation as the passage in Luke counts for nothing. They are different traditions, and therefore the *criterion of multiple context* decrees that these sayings can only belong to one of them. In other words, whenever a story was handed down in the early church in two separate traditions, it is impossible that any saying could be common to them both.

In the case of the prophet-saying in verse 24 Schmidt gives an additional reason for its deletion by appealing to the *criterion of detachability*. He points out that if verse 24 is omitted verse 23 and verse 25 would fit well together. This is true, and it would be equally easy to omit verse 22, verse 23 and verse 27 and indeed half the sayings in the gospels. Epigrammatic sayings are by their very nature detachable. The fact that they can be used equally appropriately in other contexts does not make them inappropriate in the context in which they are found.

There seems to be an inconsistency in Schmidt's comments on these sayings. First he writes as follows: 'The words ἐν τῇ πατρίδι σου (in your home area) in verse 23 will have provided the external stimulus for Luke to include at this point the well-known and probably often-quoted saying of Jesus about prophets in their home town.' In other words, the prophet-saying was a floating saying that Luke could have located anywhere, and he located it here because he found the words ἐν τῇ πατρίδι σου already present in his source. Later, however, he provides a quite different explanation. When calling into question the Nazareth location, he comments: 'This is a question that must be asked, if the words ἐν τῇ πατρίδι σου, in combination with verse 24, which occurs in Mark in another context, and the words in verse 22b which also come from Mark, are to be deleted.' This seems to imply that Luke has taken verse 22b and verse 24 from Mark 6:3f., altered them both considerably in the process, and then added a reference to the πατρίς of Jesus in verse 23 to fit in with the Markan insertions. Clearly these explanations cannot both be correct. But this does not seem to worry Schmidt. They both constitute reasons (albeit mutually inconsistent ones) for regarding these words as alien to their present context, which is his main concern.

The simplest explanation of verses 22–24 is one that Schmidt does not even consider: that both the tradition followed by Luke and the tradition followed by Mark included comments made in the synagogue about Jesus' family background and a word of Jesus about prophets not being honoured in their home area, and that these traditions both contained these two elements because that is what actually happened when Jesus visited the synagogue in Nazareth. One can understand why Schmidt does not consider this possibility. Since one of his presuppositions is the unreliability of the tradition, the suggestion that two separate traditions of a single event could in fact confirm each other must be rejected on principle.

Schmidt then proceeds to the *argument from contradiction*. He alleges that there is a difference in emphasis between Luke and the other gospels: in Mark and Matthew the Nazarenes reject Jesus, but in Luke Jesus rejects the Nazarenes. At first sight this seems an astonishing statement. In Mark and Matthew the Nazarenes are credited with unbelief; in Luke they become so angry that they try to throw Jesus down from a cliff. In the story as a whole the rejection of Jesus by the Nazarenes is far greater in Luke than in Mark and Matthew. However, in the earlier part of the story one can discern two factors that may have prompted Schmidt to define the difference in emphasis in the way he did.

First, according to Mark and Matthew the Nazarenes found Jesus' family background to be a stumbling-block to faith in him (Mark 6:3; Matt. 13:57). This statement does not occur in Luke, who simply refers to their expressions of amazement at the contrast between the gracious words of Jesus and his family background (verse 22). If the words used to describe this amazement (μαρτυρέω and θαυμάζω) are interpreted as expressing approval and admiration, then the words of Jesus in verse 23 read like a kick in the teeth to an admiring audience. But in fact these words are neutral in meaning. Μαρτυρέω means to make a statement about someone else. It can be a statement about that person's virtues (e.g. Acts 13:22), about that person's vices (e.g. Matt. 23:31) or about both together (e.g. Rom. 10:2). Similarly θαυμάζω means to be amazed either at something good (e.g. Luke 7:9) or at something bad (e.g. Luke 11:38). Thus verse 22 indicates the bewilderment of the people at the contrast between what Jesus was saying and what a carpenter's son could be expected to say. Verse 23 suggests that Jesus is reading the doubts that are already present in their minds. The words πάντως ἐρεῖτέ μοι (you will surely say to me) presuppose the presence within the synagogue community of the kind of mental stumbling-block explicitly mentioned in Mark and Matthew.

The second factor is Schmidt's interpretation of verses 25–27, in which Jesus refers to Elijah's stay at Zarephath in Sidon and Elisha's healing of Naaman the Syrian. According to Schmidt Jesus is portrayed in these verses as turning away from a stubborn, unrepentant Israel to bring salvation to the Gentiles. In Schmidt's view this understanding of Jesus' ministry may not be historically sound, but it was the understanding of the early church: Luke shared this understanding and presented Jesus' rejection of the Nazarenes as a paradigm of his general policy of turning from Israel to the Gentiles.

This argument is a good illustration of the drawbacks of dogmatism in literary criticism. The stories of Elijah and Elisha are not theological statements but illustrations and, like the parables of Jesus or any other pictorial story, they can be interpreted in a variety of ways and used in a variety of contexts. Schmidt's interpretation is allegorical – the widow of Zarephath and Naaman the Syrian represent first-century Gentiles, the unvisited widows and unhealed sufferers from leprosy represent first-century Jews. But this is not the only possible interpretation. The stories are equally appropriate in the context in which they appear in Luke, as illustrations of the principle that prophets are most appreciated away from home. By reading into these stories a fixed theological meaning, Schmidt imports into the Lukan narrative ideas that are not clearly expressed within that narrative.

In saying this, I am not denying that the stories of Elijah and Elisha would be equally appropriate in a wider context, as illustrations of the universal scope of the kingdom of God. It may be that Luke chose to place the Nazareth story at the beginning of the Galilee ministry because he saw in it an illustration of this wider principle. But if so, this would have no necessary bearing on Luke's integrity as a historian. It is one thing to say that Luke saw a significance in the words of Jesus that went beyond their immediate context; it is another thing to say that Luke deliberately modified the context to make it fit his interpretation. If the latter view is to be put forward, it needs to be buttressed by stronger evidence than a conjectural reconstruction of Luke's motivation.

The main reason for believing that the events of Luke 4:16–30 took place in Nazareth is, of course, that Luke specifically says so (verse 16). Schmidt's attempt to discredit this statement is based almost entirely on generalizations and runs as follows: (i) Stories often circulated in the early church without a precise location. (ii) If this story was circulating without a precise location, Luke could easily have located it in Nazareth because of the periodizing motives already mentioned. (iii) What we know of Luke's manner of working compels us to raise such questions. (iv) The tendency to give specific locations to gospel events, which can be seen today in the pilgrim sites of Palestine, began in New Testament times, and Luke lived in that environment. (v) The story is just as valuable if located elsewhere. (vi) Stories such as this are inherently timeless and locationless. When they were told in the course of early church worship, the hearers were not interested in their context. Introductory statements of time and place were merely a frame, and it was only the picture inside the frame that was thought to be of any value.

Let me paraphrase Schmidt's argument: the early church as a whole was unreliable, the storytellers who handed down the tradition were unreliable and Luke himself was unreliable. Therefore every statement in Luke's gospel must be treated as unreliable on principle. In a passage such as this, where there is no specific reason to question an introductory statement, doubts can always be raised by an appeal to generalizations.

Let us look at Schmidt's case in more detail. It relies first and foremost on the *argument from presuppositions*. Schmidt assumes (i) that Luke, like Mark, had no access to eyewitness information, and was dependent (apart from his knowledge of Mark) on second-hand storytellers; (ii) that these story-tellers and their audiences were not at all interested in the location of a story but only in the story itself; (iii) that Luke, like the other evangelists, felt free to add place names at will to stories that were floating in the tradition in a geographical limbo. For none of these presuppositions does he provide any objective evidence, whether here or elsewhere. Instead, he interprets each passage in the light of his presuppositions, and then appeals to his previous interpretations as evidence that his presuppositions are valid.

The lack of factual evidence for his theories is seen by Schmidt not as a liability but as an asset. In the course of his discussion of this passage he compares his methods with those of his contemporaries. He asserts that gospel criticism up to his day had concentrated mainly on the irrational elements in the gospels such as miracles.

It had tried to criticize the gospel from a factual point of view (*eine Kritik nach sachlichen Gesichtspunkten*) and neglected literary criticism. But in Schmidt's opinion it is literary criticism that is of primary importance.

It is easy to see why he believes this. Literary criticism, as Schmidt understands it, does not deal with facts and evidence but with theories and presuppositions. He describes his approach as 'a look inside the workshop of the author Luke'. Since we have no external evidence as to what went on in this workshop, the reconstruction of Luke's motives and methods is largely a matter of critical imagination. Imagination is not in itself a bad thing; we all practise it to some extent and try to picture situations in the first century as best we can. The trouble with Schmidt's approach is that, having used his imagination to create a picture of what Luke *could* have done, he then treats this picture as evidence for what Luke actually *did*.

The second weapon in Schmidt's armoury is the *argument from design*. Luke could have located this story in Nazareth, he declares, because of his desire to periodize and write biographically. It is, of course, perfectly true that Luke *could* have done this – indeed, the same argument could be used to discredit almost any statement by any person. If I tell you that the socks I am wearing were given me by my aunt as a Christmas present, you could use Schmidt's technique to cast doubt on my statement at almost every point. Christmas is an appropriate time for such a gift to be made, so my association of the gift with that season could be due to my desire to periodize. An aunt is the kind of person who might be expected to give hand-knitted socks to her nephew, so my attribution of the gift to an aunt could be due to my psychologizing. Whether or not you proceed from your analysis of what I could have done to the assumption that in fact I did so will depend on your estimate of me as a person. The same is true of Schmidt's assessment of Luke.

Schmidt regards Luke as a product of a primitive age. He cites the tendency in later centuries to find an appropriate site in Palestine for every event in the gospels, and alleges that this tendency was already operating in the first century and that Luke lived in this environment (*Lk hat in dieser Sphäre gelebt*). At first sight it seems odd to equate the situation of later centuries with Luke's situation in the first century, when many eyewitnesses of the original events were still alive. The equation is possible only because in Schmidt's opinion Luke was too incompetent a historian to consult any of these eyewitnesses and depended entirely on floating traditions and the historically worthless framework of Mark. Such incompetence was not peculiar to Luke – it was part of the environment he lived in and the air he breathed. Early Christians, Schmidt implies, were primitive people, and Luke was a typical specimen of the age he lived in.[1]

Schmidt also appeals yet again to the *criterion of detachability*. If the reference to Nazareth is deleted, he declares, the story loses none of its lustre. By 'the story' he presumably means the truncated torso that is left after he has removed all the supposed Lukan accretions. Whether the story in its truncated form shines with the same lustre as the story in its full Lukan form is a matter of opinion, and Schmidt is entitled to his opinion. Whether subsequent scholarship should take his opinion seriously is another matter.

Finally Schmidt raises a geographical question: did Nazareth have a cliff suitable for throwing someone down, as required by verse 29? On this question commentators differed in Schmidt's day and have differed ever since. Schmidt raises the matter only as a possible problem (with the word '*vielleicht*') and admits that he does not have personal knowledge of the locality. However, after quoting mutually contradictory scholarly opinions, he typically converts this possibility into a certainty. 'What all these judgments amount to is this: there are topographical difficulties that cannot be got rid of.'

Note

1   For a discussion of 'the argument from primitive culture' and its relevance to New Testament study as a whole see *Seven Pillories* chapter 3 pp. 37–54.

10

Mark 3:13–19 (*Rahmen* 109–113)

This passage describes the appointment of the twelve apostles. In Schmidt's opinion the narrative is historically worthless, and was invented either by Mark or by pre-Markan tradition to explain the existence of the apostolate. He employs several arguments to prove his case.

First comes the *argument from silence*. Schmidt lists a number of details that Mark fails to mention. The result of this silence, in his view, is a lack of vividness and clarity in the narrative. Jesus goes up a mountain, but there is no means of identifying the mountain. Is Jesus alone with his disciples or with a crowd? What is meant by the statement: 'he called to him those he wanted and they came to him'? Where were they before he called them – at the bottom of the mountain or with him higher up? Schmidt implies that any narrative that leaves such questions unanswered cannot be historical.

This argument raises an important question of methodology. It is true that there is a lack of circumstantial detail in this narrative, and that it is not clear whether the phrase 'those he wanted' refers only to the twelve or to a wider group out of which the twelve were selected. The point at issue is the explanation for this lack of detail. Schmidt attributes it to lack of historicity. But this conclusion is far from obvious. It is arguable that an invented story is more likely to be well constructed than a remembered one, which would suggest that lack of clarity is a sign of authenticity! There are in fact several possible explanations for the style of this passage. Mark could, for example, be reproducing the words of an eyewitness. Eyewitness testimony can take many forms. If I ask two different people to give me an account of a football match they attended, one may give an account full of vivid detail and the other an account containing little but the bare facts. Alternatively, Mark could be seeking to save space and to condense into a small compass a story originally told in much greater detail. Condensation can easily result in the phenomena we have in this passage. The problem with Schmidt's approach is that he does not consider literary possibilities of this sort. He works by rule of thumb – vivid detail means possible historicity; lack of detail means lack of historicity.

Schmidt then turns to an *argument from contradiction* that is also dependent on the argument from silence. The appointment of the twelve comes fairly early in Mark's narrative. Schmidt regards it as very questionable whether there could have been a fixed group of twelve apostles at such an early stage. His reasoning seems to be as follows: (i) Mark has recorded only a limited number of events in the period prior to the appointment of the twelve; (ii) therefore he must have believed that only a few events occurred during that period, and that the period was short; (iii) the selection of the twelve would necessitate a longer period than this; (iv) therefore there is an inner contradiction in Mark's narrative.

The problem with this reasoning is that it ignores the summary statements in 1:39 and 3:7–12. In 1:39 Mark states that Jesus travelled through the whole of Galilee preaching in their synagogues and casting out demons. This statement is clearly intended to summarize a considerable period, possibly of some months, and the various stories that follow (1:40–3:6) are a small sample of the many things Jesus was doing during that time. In 3:7–12 Mark describes a further seaside ministry, including many healings and exorcisms. Again Mark does not say how long all this took. There is in fact no evidence for Schmidt's assumption that the period leading up to the appointment of the twelve was conceived by Mark as being short.

However, Schmidt then goes on to squeeze even more from the argument from silence, arguing that even if we place the appointment of the twelve at a later stage in the ministry of Jesus there are still difficulties. In his view neither Mark nor any other of the evangelists portrays any development in the situation of the disciples: the act of Jesus in commissioning the twelve seems unprepared, and this means that it is timeless and suprahistorical.

It is interesting to compare this criticism with Schmidt's comment on the parallel passage in Luke (Luke 6.12–16). Luke's statement that Jesus spent the night in prayer before appointing the twelve is described as a very psychological presentation that is characteristic of Luke. As we have seen, Schmidt sees Luke's tendency to psychologize as an indication of the secondary nature of his material. But when Mark fails to psychologize and presents only bare facts, this is seen as an indication that Mark had no notion of the real sequence of events. There seems to be no way in which the evangelists could have presented their material that could not be proved to be unhistorical by one or other of these methods.

Schmidt's next weapon is the *argument from design*. He accuses Mark of being 'very schematic' in producing a catalogue of twelve names. This argument has been discussed in more detail earlier.[1] Schmidt admits that Jesus could have decided to choose twelve apostles to correspond with the twelve tribes of Israel, but still regards it as schematic (and therefore unhistorical) for Mark to give these apostles twelve names. Perhaps, if Mark had given the twelve apostles fifteen names, Schmidt might have regarded his account as possibly historical.

There follows another appeal to the *argument from design*. We know that a group of twelve apostles was in existence after the resurrection. According to Schmidt the existence of such a group would be reason enough for an account of their appointment to arise. This account could have been invented by Mark or by someone before him, but in either case it is unhistorical. Because early church curiosity *could* have led to the composition of this story, Schmidt believes that it in fact *did* so.

The principle is clear: any description of how something originated is likely to be unhistorical, because the existence of an end product is bound to lead to speculation about its origin. To test the validity of this principle, let us apply it to a more modern situation.

Suppose I read in a book that penicillin was discovered through Sir Alexander Fleming's chance observation of mould on a culture plate. This seems an unlikely origin for a major scientific discovery. It is surely more probable that the author of the book, confronted with the fact that penicillin existed, invented this obviously unhistorical story to account for its existence. Or again, suppose I read in a book that railroad sleeping cars were invented by George Mortimer Pullman. The name Pullman seems to be a descriptive term, indicating that the trains and sleeping cars concerned were designed to pull men from one place to another. Clearly the author of the book, confronted with the fact that Pullman cars existed, invented the mythical figure of George Mortimer Pullman to account for their existence.

Anyone who argued in this way about penicillin or sleeping cars could be refuted by the production of written documents. In the case of the New Testament, where such documentation is not normally available, scholars can give free rein to their scepticism.

We now turn to an *argument from contradiction*. Schmidt finds two discrepancies in this passage. First, he objects that the disciples have already been referred to in the gospel before their appointment (unless, he adds in a parenthesis, Mark was thinking of a wider circle of disciples). This parenthesis destroys the force of Schmidt's argument. When Mark refers to the disciples before the appointment of the twelve, he clearly does envisage a wider circle of disciples. As I have argued earlier, whenever the phrase 'his disciples' occurs in Mark, it means 'those disciples who were present at the time', which may be a group either larger or smaller than the twelve.[2] Had Mark used the phrase 'the twelve' earlier in the gospel, that would have constituted a genuine discrepancy, not an artificially-created one.

Second, Schmidt points out that the reference in 3:14 to sending the apostles out to preach is an anticipation of the later passage (6:7–13) in which Jesus sends the twelve out on mission. It is difficult to see why this anticipation should be regarded as a discrepancy. According to 3:14 Jesus appointed twelve men so that they could be with him and so that he could send them out to preach. In other words, his intention was that they should spend part of their time accompanying him and part of their time on mission. The later passage is thus an illustration of 3:14 rather than a contradiction of it.

Perhaps Schmidt's train of thought can be reconstructed from his comment on the parallel passage in Luke.[3] He remarks that Luke separates the mission of the twelve from their appointment, whereas in Mark the appointment-pericope also reports a sending out (*von einer Aussendung berichtet*). Schmidt seems to think that Mark 3:14 contains not a statement of intent but a report of an actual mission. Mark's words are as follows: καὶ ἐποίησεν δώδεκα, οὓς καὶ ἀποστόλους ὠνόμασεν, ...ἵνα ἀποστέλλῃ αὐτοὺς κηρύσσειν ....[4] How Schmidt can interpret a ἵνα-clause as a report of an actual mission passes my comprehension. Nor can I understand how Schmidt's readers could have accepted such an interpretation. Perhaps they were too shell-shocked by his barrage of alleged discrepancies to muster the energy to look up the passages concerned and check whether Mark's words meant what Schmidt claimed they meant.

Schmidt then employs the *criterion of detachability*. The account of the choosing of the twelve could be omitted from its Markan context, and indeed from the gospel as a whole, without anything being lost. This assertion extends the criterion of detachability beyond its normal range. Normally the criterion is used to identify what Schmidt considers to be a floating fragment that belonged to the tradition as a whole but not to its Markan context. Here it is used to identify a story that is adjudged not to belong to the gospel tradition at all. As a literary judgment this is highly questionable. Certainly the story is detachable from its immediate context, in that verse 20 could easily follow verse 12. But if it were omitted from the gospel altogether, the later references to the twelve (e.g. 6:7; 10:41; 14:17) would be unintelligible.

Schmidt justifies his assertion in a paragraph that is worth quoting in full, since it illustrates the attitude of mind that lies behind so much of his criticism.

> By way of appendix let us make a brief comment on our judgment that this event is unhistorical. Such a criticism does not destroy anything of significance. The story can be removed not only from its present context but also from the gospel as a whole without anything being lost. The decisive thing is this: the twelve men here named are for us simply names. Only some of them are known to us from other stories as somewhat clearly defined personalities. Basically the whole thing is a list that has no proper inner life (*eine Liste ohne rechtes inneres Leben*).

This comment reveals a lot about Schmidt's approach to literary criticism. He seems to think that he can measure the amount of life in a gospel story by a calculation based on the amount of background information provided. He would presumably regard a war memorial as lifeless and meaningless unless detailed information were provided about the personality of each person named. Throughout the book subjective opinions of this sort are put forward as *ex cathedra* pronouncements. Mark's account of the appointment of the twelve, and the list of names he gives, have fascinated scholars through the centuries, and many books have been written about them. But these count for nothing in the face of Schmidt's boundless confidence in his own literary judgment. Mark's account is lifeless, because the oracle has spoken.

Notes

1 See Chapter 2 ('The argument from design') 25f. and the references in footnotes 17–20.
2 See pp. 38f.
3 *Rahmen* 164.
4 The words οὓς καὶ ἀποστόλους ὠνόμασεν are omitted in some manuscripts.

11

Luke 10:1–12 (*Rahmen* 166–169)

This passage describes the sending out on mission of 70 (or 72) disciples. Schmidt employs four arguments to prove that Luke's account is unhistorical.

He begins with the *argument from contradiction*. According to Luke 10:1 Jesus appointed 'another group of 70(72)' (ἑτέρους ἑβδομήκοντα [δύο]). What does Luke mean by 'another group'? Virtually all commentators before Schmidt, whether ancient or modern, had assumed that the implied contrast was with the sending out of the twelve in the previous chapter (9:1–6). But Schmidt (following B. Weiss) prefers to see a reference back to 9:52, where Jesus sent messengers to arrange accommodation in a Samaritan village. He recognizes that this limited mission to arrange accommodation does not provide a proper parallel to the extended mission of the 70(72), and calls this an incongruity (*Inkonzinnität*) that cannot be eliminated by the spiritualizing exegesis that the mission of the 70 concerned the provision of accommodation for Jesus in the human heart. The reason for the incongruity, he believes, is that Luke is here conflating two sources – the special source he has been following in 9:51–56 and the source 'Q' that he follows in the mission address in 10:2–16. On this theory, Luke took the word ἑτέρους from the special source, where it referred to another set of messengers like the ones in 9:52; but at the same time he had a picture in his mind of the contrast with the twelve apostles and of the great number of labourers required in the harvest field (10:2). The confusion of these two ideas in the text is due to the confusion in Luke's mind.

The portrayal of Luke as a confused author, taking over a word from one source and trying unsuccessfully to combine it with a mental picture taken from another, is consistent with Schmidt's low opinion of Luke's ability in general. But it is not justified by the evidence. The

vast majority of commentators see in the word ἑτέρους a reference
back to the mission of the twelve, and this makes good sense. The
incongruity is not in the text but in Schmidt's offbeat interpretation.

There then follows an *argument from design*. Although it is impossible to decide with certainty whether the number 70 or 72 appeared
in Luke's original text, in either case Luke's presentation is regarded
as schematic, since both 70 and 72 are schematic numbers in Jewish
tradition. The fact that Luke records a schematic number does not
mean that he invented it. Schmidt's opinion is that a body of 70(72)
men did exist in the early church; an attempt was made to explain its
existence by inventing the story of their appointment by Jesus; and
Luke has latched on to this tradition.

It seems somewhat harsh to accuse Luke of schematism if, as
Schmidt believes, he did not invent the number 70(72) but took it
over from the tradition. Nor can this charge be levelled against the
tradition either, if it was simply reflecting the existence of a genuine
group of 70(72) men. The people who are really guilty of schematism,
if we accept Schmidt's theory, are the people (whoever they were)
who appointed the 70(72) in the first place.

Matthew and Mark do not refer to the 70(72) and relate only a
mission by the twelve; but in Schmidt's opinion they are just as
schematic as Luke. He believes that Jesus did in fact address his
mission teaching to a wider group than the twelve. Matthew and
Mark's limitation of this teaching to the twelve was due to 'an
unhistorical schematism' that needed to be criticized, even though in
offering his criticism Luke did not escape from the use of schematic
numbers.[1]

Schmidt's criticism of Matthew and Mark is dependent on the
argument from silence. The logic of his argument seems to be as follows:

(a)   Matthew and Mark both aim to give a complete picture of the
total ministry of Jesus.

(b)   Matthew and Mark report only one occasion on which disciples were sent out on mission.

(c)   Therefore, in the view of Matthew and Mark, this was the only
mission that took place during the ministry of Jesus.

The weakness of this argument lies in its major premiss. Matthew
and Mark did not aim to present a complete picture of the ministry
of Jesus. The various statements of time ('after some days' and the
like) and the historical summaries (*Sammelberichte*) that are scattered
throughout both gospels are clearly designed to create an impression

of a lengthy ministry, the details of which are largely unrecorded. The aim of the evangelists was to provide a representative sample of each facet of that ministry, with each recorded event representing many unrecorded events. The one recorded instance in Matthew and Mark of Jesus sending out disciples on mission could have been a unique event and could equally well have been one among several such missions. The argument from silence is of no value when applied to books as selective as the gospels.

Schmidt's decisive argument against the historicity of Luke's account is another *argument from silence*. There is no mention of a group of 70 or 72 disciples in the gospels apart from this one passage in Luke. Schmidt alleges that, had such a group existed in the time of Jesus, its existence must have produced reverberations in the gospel record. But his use of the words 'college' (*Kollegium*) and 'circle' (*Kreis*) to describe the 70(72) begs the question. There is no suggestion in Luke that these men formed a permanent group analogous to the twelve. If they were an *ad hoc* group, formed for this particular mission only and then disbanded, we should not expect any further reference to them. Perhaps the fact that Schmidt had recently served in the army made him feel subconsciously that missions of this sort could be accomplished only by a properly constituted body under a permanent command structure.

In fact, the argument from silence militates against Schmidt's theory as much as it does against Luke's text. If, as Schmidt believes, there was a permanent body of 70(72) men in the early church, including such figures as Stephen, Philip and Barnabas, why is there no mention of such a body in the Acts of the Apostles? The logic of the argument from silence, if consistently applied, seems to require the conclusion that this body of men is a total fabrication. The fabrication theory had been advocated in Schmidt's day by scholars such as Wellhausen, but Schmidt rejects it as 'not totally excluded but less probable'. He is apparently willing to accept the total silence of Acts, but unwilling to accept the comparative silence of the gospels. What he never seems to question is the validity of the argument from silence.

The final appeal is to the *criterion of multiple context*. Jesus's charge to the 70(72) is, according to Schmidt, an unmistakable doublet of the charge to the twelve in Mark 6 and Matthew 10. It is a pity, as I have said earlier, that Schmidt has not consistently followed the logic of his own scepticism about doublet theories.[2] If we take this scepti-

cism seriously, and are therefore open to the possibility that the
mission of the twelve and the mission of the 70(72) could both be
historical, would we not expect the charges given to these two groups
to exhibit points of similarity? If someone prepared for confirmation
by a particular clergyman in 1992 and someone prepared for confirmation by the same clergyman in 1993 were to compare notes of their
confirmation classes, there could well be agreements in ideas and
wording between the two sets of notes as well as some differences.
Would this lead to the conclusion that the two people must have been
confirmed on the same day? If such an argument would be regarded
as ridiculous when applied to the ministry of a modern clergyman why
should it be regarded as acceptable when applied to the ministry of
Jesus?

Moreover, even if we accept the theory that, in reporting the charge
to the 70(72), Luke has collected sayings from 'Q' or elsewhere and
placed them in what seemed to him to be a suitable context, this would
have no bearing on the historicity of the mission itself, any more than
the theory that Paul's speech at Athens in Acts 17 is a Lukan
fabrication necessarily implies that Paul never visited Athens.

Notes

1   For the text of Schmidt's argument, see Chapter 2 note 19.
2   See Chapter Six pp. 79–81.

12

Mark 6:30 (*Rahmen* 178–180)

Mark 6:30 states that 'the apostles gathered round Jesus and reported to him all they had done and taught'(NIV). In its Markan context this verse follows the account of the sending out of the twelve on mission (6:7–13), after the parenthesis about the death of John the Baptist (6:14–29). Schmidt's theory, however, is that the original form of this verse referred to disciples of John the Baptist or messengers (apostles) sent by them, and that Mark took over these words from the tradition and gave them a new reference to the disciples of Jesus. This argument is something of a *tour de force* even by Schmidt's standards and is worth examining in detail.

He starts with the *argument from silence*. The situation is not clearly portrayed, he alleges, because information is missing. When did the disciples return? Where was Jesus while they were away? What did he do during this time? Schmidt implies that we cannot have what he calls 'an objection-free portrayal of the situation' unless all these details are given and the narrative is several times as long. As usual, he treats conciseness as a sign of lack of historicity.

His second argument springs from his *theory of Markan artlessness*. Mark's insertion of the death of John the Baptist between the sending out of the twelve and their return suggests to Schmidt that there is a hiatus in Mark's sources. The idea that Mark could have deliberately inserted the John the Baptist story at this point, as an artistic device to give the illusion of the passage of time, is not even considered. As we have seen, Schmidt believes Mark to be artless and unsophisticated and incapable of such devices[1]. Rather, the insertion is seen as an indication that 6:7–13 (the sending out of the twelve), 6:14–29 (the death of John the Baptist) and 6:31–44 (the crossing of the lake and the feeding of the five thousand) were all originally independent, and 6:30 represents Mark's attempt to relate these independent stories to each other.

Schmidt then turns to the *argument from textual tradition*. The vast majority of older manuscripts read: καὶ ἀπήγγειλαν αὐτῷ πάντα ὅσα ἐποίησαν καὶ ὅσα ἐδίδαξαν – 'and they reported to him everything both what they had done and what they had taught'. However, ΑΓ and many later manuscripts insert a καί between πάντα and ὅσα. This reading can be translated so as to give the same sense as the majority reading. But it is also possible to refer πάντα to the death of John the Baptist – 'and they reported to him everything (*sc.* about John's death) and what they had done and taught (*sc.* on mission).' Schmidt observes that this reading could be a later alteration, but it could also represent Mark's original text and thus give us a clue to Mark's editorial activity.

He finds a further clue in a reading peculiar to the Sinaitic Syriac version, which alters the plurals in the latter part of the verse into singulars – 'they told Jesus everything *he* had done and taught.' Schmidt argues that the Syriac word for 'apostles' could refer to messengers from John's disciples, and the meaning could then be that messengers came from John's disciples and told Jesus all that John had done and taught. He admits that this cannot represent the original text of Mark: if disciples of John had come to Jesus, they would have told him about the death of their master, not about his deeds and teaching. Nevertheless, he detects in this variant the clue to the prehistory of this verse.

According to Schmidt's reconstruction the account of John's death as Mark received it will have ended as follows: 'they (the representatives of the disciples of John) told Jesus about the death of their master.'[2] Mark has altered these words into the form we now have in 6:30, because he wished to establish a connection with the account of the sending out of the twelve earlier in the chapter. The fact that this involved a change both of subject and of object – a new identity for the 'apostles' and a new content to their message – would presumably not have bothered Mark; he was, one assumes, either too stupid to notice or too unscrupulous to care. If this theory is accepted, the key to Mark's editorial activity is found in *two* textual variants. One (the reading of ΑΓ and later manuscripts) is regarded by almost all other scholars as a secondary alteration. The other (the reading peculiar to the Sinaitic Syriac) even Schmidt concedes cannot represent the original text of Mark.

At first sight one wonders why Schmidt should go to such extraordinary lengths to cast doubt on a verse that reads perfectly smoothly as it stands. But the reason becomes clear in his final paragraph:

> What is the result of our considerations? Given the difficulty of such questions involving compositional technique, the result is not clearly defined. The certainty with which expositors here reach verdicts of a much less complicated kind springs from the fact that, in spite of some attempts to move in another direction, it is generally presupposed that the pericopes follow one another in a self-contained sequence. It has already become clear again and again that there is no such sequence. Mark compiled his stories from internal and external motives. We do not know these motives, and can demonstrate only a small part of them. Purely literary considerations help us in this task. What seems to me to be important is this modest result: the view that 6:7ff. and 6:30ff. were originally linked by a reference to the sending out and return of the disciples is unproven.

In this paragraph Schmidt reveals the reason for his procedure. He is unwilling to recognize an original link between 6:7–13 and 6:30 because that would go against the basic presupposition of his book. Therefore some argument or other, however far-fetched, must be found to cast doubt on this link and create a general atmosphere of uncertainty.

When I read Schmidt's discussion of this verse, it leaves me with a sense of bewilderment. This is not because of the argument itself – I can understand that he may have felt compelled to argue in the way he did by the pressure of his presuppositions. What puzzles me is the fact that a book containing arguments of this sort has been regarded for most of the twentieth century as one of the foundation pillars of our modern understanding of the gospels. If the foundation is like this, what hope is there for the superstructure? Admittedly Schmidt's argument at this point is more far-fetched than usual. But the difference is in degree rather than in kind. The basic features of his technique – the appeals to presupposition and conjecture with only the flimsiest of evidential support – are present in equal measure throughout the book.

Notes

1   See the section in chapter 1 p. 13.
2   Schmidt notes that according to Matthew 14:12 the disciples of John did tell
    Jesus about the death of their master. But he believes that Matthew is totally
    dependent on Mark at this point, and therefore Matthew's text, being a
    deliberate alteration of Mark, cannot be used as evidence for pre-Markan
    tradition. Since Matthew does not place the mission of the twelve at the same
    stage in the narrative as Mark, he has to substitute something for Mark's
    reference to the return of the twelve. In so doing, Schmidt believes, he may have
    produced (presumably by coincidence) a text that corresponds to Mark's
    original source.

13

Mark 9:33-37 – (*Rahmen* 229–231)

This passage is set by Mark in the context of a journey through Galilee towards Jerusalem, in the course of which Jesus tried to prepare his disciples for his death and resurrection (9:30–32). When they reached a house in Capernaum Jesus asked them what they had been discussing on the way. They were ashamed to admit they had been discussing who was the greatest. Jesus then summoned the twelve and uttered various sayings, using a child as a visual aid.

Schmidt regards the framework of this passage as historically worthless, and argues (i) that the reference to Capernaum may have been added to the pre-Markan tradition at some stage in its development; (ii) that the dispute story was not originally tied to any particular time and that Mark has located it here for topical reasons; (iii) that the passage is not a unity: verses 33f., 35 and 36f. were originally separate units, and have been put together either by Mark or by pre-Markan tradition. Let us look at these arguments one by one.

(i) The reference to Capernaum falls foul of the *argument from contradiction*. Schmidt describes it as peculiar (*sonderbar*), because Mark's statement in 9:30 that Jesus was travelling through Galilee leads us to expect him to be either further south than Capernaum by this time or further east. As is often the case, Schmidt's criticism is in fact more peculiar than the text he is criticizing. The starting-point for the journey through Galilee, according to Mark's narrative, was the 'high mountain' of transfiguration (9:2). The location of this mountain is disputed. The traditional site, Mount Tabor, some 10 miles south-west of the Sea of Galilee, is less than 2000 feet above sea level. A spur of Mount Hermon (12 miles north-east of Caesarea Philippi) or one of the three mountains of more than 4000 feet south-east of Caesarea Philippi have been suggested as possible sites. A journey towards Jerusalem from any of these could well pass through Capernaum, even if we assume (as Schmidt appears to) that travelling through Galilee must mean travelling in a straight line with no detours.

However, Schmidt's belief that the reference to Capernaum is 'completely out of keeping with the central theme of Mark's narrative' does lead him to one positive conclusion – that Mark has not invented this reference but drawn it from tradition. He does not, of course, mean by this that it is historically reliable. He hints at the 'possibility' that the story referred originally simply to a house and that at some stage in the tradition someone assumed the house must be Peter's house in Capernaum. He provides no evidence for this 'possibility'. He relies presumably on the *argument from presuppositions*: since the pre-Markan tradition was unreliable, and early church storytellers added details such as this at the drop of a hat, such details should be regarded as unreliable on principle, even if there is no evidence to suggest this.

(ii) With regard to the context of the conversation, Schmidt admits that the words 'on the way' (v. 33) suit the context in which Mark has placed them. But the idea that this might be the correct context falls foul of the *argument from design*. Schmidt argues that the dispute story (unless it was always an isolated story) may have stood at an earlier stage in the tradition in a different context. Mark, he asserts, has introduced it here because it is appropriate to this section of the gospel, which is concerned with Jesus and his disciples. The logic of this assertion seems to be that, wherever a story is appropriate to its Markan context, it must be Mark who has artificially made it so.

Again, we may test the validity of this argument by applying it to a more modern situation. What was the original context of the words of Sir Winston Churchill, 'Never in the field of human conflict was so much owed by so many to so few'? There were a number of situations in the Second World War, and in the other periods of history about which Churchill is known to have written, to which these words would have been appropriate. Therefore, if I read in a book that they were spoken with reference to the Battle of Britain in 1940, I may well be tempted to argue that the author of the book has placed them in this context for topical reasons – the author's concern was to glorify those who took part in the Battle of Britain, and the Churchill quotation was appropriate for that purpose. In practice, this kind of argument is not used as often in respect of contemporary history as it is used in respect of the gospels. The reason for this is the availability of documentary evidence. In the case of the Churchill quotation, my sceptical doubts could be laid to rest by consulting Hansard, the official record of British parliamentary debates; but for the teaching of Jesus no Hansard is available. As a result, the arguments of sceptical New Testament scholars acquire a certain plausibility. Even though evidence to support their arguments is lacking, there is equally no evidence to refute them.

(iii) With regard to the internal unity of the passage Schmidt employs a number of arguments. Again he begins with the *argument from contradiction*. According to 9:33 Jesus asked his travelling companions what they were discussing on the way. The verse says 'he asked them' without stating the identity of 'them' ; but the previous pericope (9:30–32) consists of teaching given by Jesus to 'his disciples', and it is fair to assume that by 'them' Mark means 'his disciples'. On receiving no reply to his question, Jesus sat down, summoned the twelve and talked to them. In Schmidt's opinion this sequence of events does not make sense. How can Jesus summon his disciples if they are already present? He therefore suggests two possibilities: either Mark has combined two separate units of tradition, or he is seeking to create a solemn impression with a 'somewhat clumsy' style.

The assumption behind this argument is that any reference to the disciples must be a reference to the twelve. But if we look at Mark's gospel as a whole, this is patently not the case. Jesus was often accompanied by other people in addition to the twelve. Mark refers in 4:10 to 'those who were around Jesus including the twelve', and in 15:40f. to a group of women who travelled with Jesus in Galilee and others who accompanied him to Jerusalem. On the other hand, in 9:14–29 the term 'his disciples' includes only some of the twelve, since Peter, James and John were absent on the mount of transfiguration during the events described. In the light of Mark's usage elsewhere, the group of travelling companions referred to in verses 33f. can be pictured as being either greater or smaller than the twelve.

The general impression created by Mark's gospel is that Jesus was often accompanied by a large number of followers, but that from time to time he separated off the twelve as a distinct group. This occurred when he sent them out on mission (6:7), when he wished to impart some special teaching (9:35; 10:32) or for special occasions such as the passover meal (14:17). Such a picture makes good sense, and Schmidt has no solid grounds for questioning it.

There then follows an *argument from silence*. The parallel passage in Matthew contains no equivalent to verse 35. Schmidt declares that this omission is 'worthy of note' (*beachtenswert*), without telling us wherein the noteworthiness lies. In view of the substantial differences between the accounts in Mark and Matthew it is clear that, even if we accept Markan priority, Matthew was following other sources besides Mark at this point. Schmidt himself comments that the Matthew passage is partly reminiscent of Mark and partly of Luke. Moreover, even if we regard the absence of a parallel to verse 35 as due to deliberate omission by Matthew, the significance of such an omission is far from obvious. However much scholars may wish to dogmatize about the reasons for omissions, those reasons are rarely clear-cut. Did Matthew wish to correct Mark's style, did he think the event described (the summoning of the twelve) never occurred, did he wish to save space in his manuscript for what he felt to be more important matters, or was he combining material from various sources and presenting a new version in his own words? Since we have no evidence to decide this question, our answer will be a matter of conjecture, and will probably reflect our pre-existing view of Matthew's literary technique. But even if we think we can work out Matthew's reason for omitting this verse, that would still tell us nothing about how the words came to be in Mark's text in the first place, which is the context in which Schmidt raises the issue and seems to regard as significant.

Equally irrelevant is Schmidt's appeal to the *criterion of multiple context*. The other 'noteworthy' feature of Mark 9:35, he asserts, is that this saying occurs also in Luke 9:48b. Again he does not specify in what respect it is noteworthy, nor is it immediately obvious. Luke 9:48 forms part of the Lukan parallel to Mark 9:33–37. There is a slight variation in order, in that the saying in Luke comes at the end of the pericope (after the introduction of the child) rather than in the middle of the pericope as in Mark. More significantly, the two sayings in Mark and Luke differ almost totally in content. Mark 9:35b reads: 'If anyone wants to be first, he must be last of all and servant of all.' Luke 9:48b reads: 'The least among you all is the greatest.' The only thing these two sayings have in common is the same general theme. To call them variants of a single original saying is possible only if one believes as a matter of dogma that Jesus could have uttered only one saying on any given theme.

Then follows an *argument from textual tradition*. Schmidt points out that Codex Bezae (D) contains the words 'he sat down and called the twelve', but omits the saying that follows these words. We are not told the significance of this fact. Even a scholar whose approach to textual criticism is as eclectic as Schmidt's can hardly be claiming that the reading of this one manuscript represents what Mark wrote. Perhaps he thinks that any textual variant, however trivial, can serve to cast doubt on the text. The argument seems to run as follows: the scribe who copied out Codex Bezae must have omitted these words because he felt they were worthy of omission, and the fact that he felt this proves how poorly constructed Mark's text is. The modern equivalent of this argument would be the statement that a book must be bad if one of its reviewers says it is bad.

Finally, Schmidt applies the *criterion of multiple context* to the passage as a whole. Parallels to all the sayings in this passage can be found in Huck's *Synopsis*. The fact that many of these parallel sayings occur in other contexts is described by Schmidt as important (*wichtig*). It leads him to the conclusion that this passage consists of isolated sayings that have been collected and furnished with an introduction either by Mark or by pre-Markan tradition. As is often the case, this theory is first put forward as a 'possibility', but the ensuing discussion as to whether the compilation was done by Mark or his predecessors treats it as though it were a fact.

We may test Schmidt's theory by examining the parallels to Mark 9:37 listed in Huck's *Synopsis*. Mark 9:37 reads: 'Whoever welcomes one such child in my name welcomes me; and whoever welcomes me welcomes the one who sent me.' The parallel passages in Matthew (18:1–5) and Luke (9:46–48) both contain a version of this saying set in the same context. In addition, in Matthew 10:40 Jesus says to his disciples: 'anyone who welcomes you welcomes me, and whoever welcomes me welcomes the one who sent me.' These words form part of the address of Jesus to the twelve when sending them out on mission. In Luke somewhat similar words occur in Jesus's address to the 70(72) missioners (10:16): 'Whoever listens to you listens to me, and whoever rejects you rejects me; and whoever rejects me rejects the one who sent me.' There are also parallel sayings in John's gospel: 'Whoever believes in me believes not in me but in the one who sent me; and whoever sees me sees the one who sent me' (12:44f.); 'Whoever receives someone I send receives me, and whoever receives me receives the one who sent me' (13:20).

The common theme in all these verses is that what is done to children or disciples is done to Jesus, and what is done to Jesus is done

to the one who sent him. This theme is applied in different ways –
what is done may be welcoming or rejecting, seeing or believing. The
recipients are children in Mark 9:37 and parallels, disciples in the
other passages. There are two possible ways of explaining these
variations.

One explanation is that Jesus employed this way of speaking on one
occasion only. He spoke either about children or about disciples. He
spoke either about welcoming or about rejection or about seeing and
believing. On this theory it is the task of the exegete to decide which
of the variants represents most closely the single original saying, and
which of the contexts in the gospels (if any) is the single original
context.

The alternative explanation is that this was a favourite motif of
Jesus, which he developed in various ways in various contexts. On this
theory Jesus was like a musician composing variations on a theme; the
various sayings are not contradictory but complementary. The advantage of this theory is that it corresponds with the way in which creative
artists (whether in words or in music) habitually work.

It would be interesting to apply Schmidt's technique to Bach's
Mass in B minor, in which the same music is used for two choruses –
Gratias agimus and *Dona nobis pacem*. A disciple of Schmidt would
have to ask which of these was the original setting and which was a
later interpolation. Again, there is a close parallel between the *Cruci-
fixus* and Bach's Easter Cantata No. 12. If we follow Schmidt's
principles, we should have to ask which of these two contexts is
authentic and which is due to the work of a later editor. In fact, seven
out of the 25 movements in the B minor Mass have close parallels
elsewhere in Bach's published work. Schmidt's approach fails to
recognize that great artists constantly repeat the same motifs in
different contexts. The same is true of painting. The paintings from
Picasso's blue period are not to be regarded *à la Schmidt* as variant
versions of a single painting, but as complementary outworkings of a
motif in Picasso's mind. It is a mystery why repetition with variations
should be regarded as a normal and natural procedure by critics of
other art forms, but as an abnormal and unnatural procedure by critics
of the gospels.

Part III

14

The Background to Schmidt's *Rahmen*

Schmidt's was a pioneering work, which did not belong to any school. Though regarded today as one of the founders of Form Criticism, together with Martin Dibelius and Rudolf Bultmann, Schmidt worked independently of these men and his approach differs in some ways from theirs. Nor is he dependent on the scholars of the previous generation in any slavish way. When he quotes other scholars, it is more often than not in order to disagree with them. Nevertheless, he was a child of his time, and it is important to see him against his historical background.

This can be seen by referring to three of Schmidt's predecessors – William Wrede, Albert Schweitzer and Julius Wellhausen. These men differed considerably from each other in their opinions, and Schmidt could not be called a disciple of any of them. However, despite their differences, they exhibit certain common ways of thinking and arguing that were in the air at the time when Schmidt's ideas were taking shape in his mind. We shall concentrate not so much on the distinctive opinions of these scholars as on the methods of argument they employ, many of which are common to all three of them and are also prominent in Schmidt's *Rahmen*. I hope in this way to reveal something of the methodological debt Schmidt owed to his predecessors.

i) William Wrede

Wrede's book *The Messianic Secret in the Gospels*, was published in 1901, 18 years before the *Rahmen*.[1] Wrede concentrates on those passages in the gospels (and in Mark in particular) where Jesus tells people (or demons) to be quiet. He also discusses other passages containing a suggestion of secrecy or mystery – where Jesus talks to the disciples on their own, or the disciples are portrayed as unable to understand Jesus' teaching. In the first part of the book Wrede's aim is to prove that all these passages are unhistorical, and that Mark, the earliest of the evangelists, 'no longer has any real idea of the historical life of Jesus.'[2] Having established this, he then sets out to discover why the unhistorical concept of a messianic secret was imposed upon the tradition.

The solution Wrede eventually endorses is reached by a process of elimination; he acknowledges it to be experimental, and it has in fact failed to gain general acceptance over the years.[3] The main importance of Wrede's work – the reason why Christopher Tuckett can write that 'in terms of method, the influence of his book has continued right up to the present day'[4] – lies in the former part of the book, in the demolition techniques that Wrede uses to undermine Mark's credibility as a historical source. So far as Schmidt's *Rahmen* is concerned, his closest link with Wrede lies not in the sphere of ideas or theology, but in the application of the same demolition techniques to a different area of gospel study.

Four arguments in particular underlie Wrede's presentation.

a)   The argument from presuppositions

Wrede's primary criterion for deciding what material is unhistorical is rationalist dogma. Any narrative that contains any supernatural element such as miracle or prophecy must *ipso facto* be judged to be unhistorical. This consideration, Wrede asserts, must be compelling for 'all those who recognize only historical standards in Gospel research'. He writes:

> Mark actually has a large share of unhistorical narratives in his Gospel. No critical theologian believes his report on the baptism of Jesus, the raising of Jairus's daughter, the miraculous feedings, the walking of Jesus on the water, the transfiguration, or the conversation of the angel with the women at the tomb, in the sense in which he records them.[5]

This criterion is applied rigorously throughout the book. The healing of the man with leprosy (1:40ff.), we are told, 'cannot be regarded as a historical account by historical research, which does not recognize miracles in the strict sense.'[6] As to the stories about casting out demons, 'the critics naturally cannot take Mark's items of information in the sense they originally had.'[7] Some of the sayings relating to the slowness of understanding of the disciples 'are completely dependent on the preceding narrative, which is conceived as strictly miraculous, and . . . are thus at once characterized as fabrications.'[8] With regard to the injunction to secrecy after the transfiguration (9:9), Wrede asks: 'Will a saying be historical which only has its place in the story of the transfiguration and which moreover places in Jesus' mouth foreknowledge of his resurrection?'[9] The same principle applies to the passion predictions: 'It is obvious that these passion predictions are schematic, and contain things that Jesus cannot have known, and in particular that Jesus cannot have prophesied the absolute miracle of an immediate return to life.'[10]

These statements are clear and consistent and their effect is drastic. If every narrative that portrays Jesus as performing miracles, or as having knowledge that could come only from God, is to be adjudged unhistorical on principle, Wrede's task of demolishing Mark's credibility is half accomplished by virtue of this criterion alone. It is important to realize that the basis of the criterion is pure dogma. Wrede's judgment is not drawn from the narrative but imposed upon it. C.S. Lewis, in an address to theological students, drew attention to the limitations of this kind of dogmatism:

> I do not here want to discuss whether the miraculous is possible. I only want to point out that this is a purely philosophical question. Scholars, as scholars, speak on it with no more authority than anyone else. The canon, 'If miraculous, unhistorical' is one they bring to their study of the texts, not one they have learned from it. If one is speaking of authority, the united authority of all the Biblical critics in the world counts here for nothing. On this they speak simply as men; men obviously influenced by, and perhaps insufficiently critical of, the spirit of the age they grew up in.[11]

Interestingly, Wrede claims that his view of Mark's gospel is similar to the view of John's gospel held by 'unbiased scientific criticism'.[12] Clearly he regards himself as a practitioner of unbiased scientific criticism, and seems unaware of the extent to which his approach is controlled by philosophical dogma. He is so busy trying to correct the bias in his brother's eye that he cannot see the bias in his own.

Schmidt's *Rahmen* is not on the whole concerned with the historicity of the gospel stories but only with their framework, and therefore is not controlled by rationalist dogma in the same way as Wrede's book. What is common to both works, however, is the methodology – the belief in the propriety of deciding historical questions by an appeal to presuppositions. Schmidt's presuppositions may differ from Wrede's, but the technique is the same.

b)   *The argument from silence*

Wrede makes use of the argument from silence in two main ways: as a means of casting doubt on the historicity of stories in the gospels; and as a means of casting doubt on the theories of other scholars.

(i)   Silence and historicity

Mark records various occasions on which Jesus forbade people to publicize what they had experienced, but does not explain Jesus's reasons for these prohibitions. This seems to Wrede very odd. 'Would we not expect occasionally a hint of such motives?' he asks.[13] Mark's silence on this issue seems to him to reflect the nature of Mark's authorship as a whole: Mark records brief, hasty words of Jesus with a short comment on the impression they made, sudden changes of location and the unexplained appearance and disappearance of crowds and disciples; but the psychological and other motivations which alone could give palpable shape to these events are lacking, because Mark never thought about the matter. Wrede concludes:

> Thus the appearance of Jesus and of the other persons in the drama frequently gives the impression of something hasty, shadowy, almost phantasmal.[14]

A case in point is Peter's confession. Why is it, Wrede asks, that the portrayal of the disciples as slow to understand in 8:15ff. is followed almost immediately in 8:27ff. by Peter's confession? If the narrator was aware of the significance of this transformation, some hint would have been appropriate as to whether the change was sudden or gradual.[15] The story of the gradual opening of the eyes of the blind man that lies between the two stories in Mark's narrative (8:22–26) would probably not have counted as such a hint in Wrede's eyes, since it is an indirect hint rather than a logical one. Any narrative that reports actions without providing logical explanations for those actions cannot, in Wrede's opinion, be historical.

It is not only Mark's silence about motivation that seems significant to Wrede. Characteristic of his approach is what may be called the nit-picking style of argument. This consists in taking a story that reads perfectly naturally as it stands, and finding fault with it on the grounds that Mark does not include sufficient explanatory details. A good example is the story of the Syro-Phoenician woman in Mark 7:24–30.[16] Jesus enters a house in the region of Tyre and Sidon and wishes to remain hidden. Wrede asks why a place of hiding is needed in a strange land. Granted that, according to Mark 3:8, Jesus was known to many of the inhabitants of the area, what is the use of a purely temporary hiding-place, and why does Jesus hide here and not hide in other places? In reply to B. Weiss, who suggests a possible reason, he objects that Mark does not tell us this reason. In other words, wherever Mark states a fact without providing an explanation, it is illegitimate to try to conjecture the explanation, but legitimate to use the absence of an explanation as proof that the story is unhistorical. Wrede then refers to the disparity (*Missverhältnis*) between the region of Tyre and Sidon and 'a' house. Presumably he means that the one reference is definite and the other indefinite. The story could be historical, one assumes, only if Mark had given all the details of the house – e.g. that they went to the house of Aristion in the village of Naboth about 23 kilometres north-east of Tyre, Aristion being Peter and Andrew's second cousin on their mother's side. In the absence of such details Wrede states that the story reads like a fairy tale of a Spanish prince wandering in disguise in French territory. The basic proof that the narrative is unhistorical is Mark's lack of '*Anschaulichkeit*' (vivid detail). We have come across several examples of this kind of argument in Schmidt's *Rahmen*. Perhaps it reflects a general feeling among scholars of the period that the important thing in a narrative is the volume of factual information, and that conciseness is a sign of historical ineptitude.

(ii) Silence and modern reconstructions

Again and again Wrede opposes the interpretations of other scholars on the grounds that there is no express statement in Mark to support their interpretation. This is particularly true of attempts by scholars to reconstruct the motives of Jesus. The logic of Wrede's argument is difficult to follow. If, as he alleges, failure to attribute motives to Jesus is a consistent element in Mark's style, there is unlikely to be explicit support in Mark for the existence of any motive of any kind. If modern scholars conjecture that Jesus may have had such and such a motive, the absence of any direct reference to that motive in Mark should be seen as a normal feature of Mark's style, not as a reason for opposing that conjecture. However, Wrede finds this argument very useful in rejecting the views of scholars he disagrees with.

For example, the suggestion that 'Son of Man' was an enigmatic title, which Jesus could have chosen for that very reason, is rejected on the grounds that Mark does not explicitly say this. 'Nowhere is there even a note telling us that people were brought up sharply by this title and did not understand it, or that Jesus chose it with a definite purpose in mind.'[17] The suggestion that Jesus was trying to avoid a false belief in a political Messiah is similarly rejected on the grounds that 'the narrator has not touched upon it by any direct allusion.'[18] The suggestion that Jesus was an educator is rejected on the grounds that Mark does not mention any process of development that would deserve the name of education. 'It can be surmised only by those who consider it right to fill in the gaps between the extant data with subjective notions of their own or link up what the narrator has not linked up in any recognizable way. . . . Where do we find passages in Mark which clearly delineate the educational point of view?'[19] Wrede pours scorn on those critics who attach great importance to Peter's confession, and points out 'how very much the brevity and poverty of the actual statements made by Mark contrast with the ideas discovered here by exegetes and critics of the most varied kinds.' He admits that historians are not limited to 'the bare text of an unpretentious account', but alleges that the conditions that would make imaginative interpretation legitimate are not present in this case.[20] In practice, there seem to be few cases where he does regard such interpretation as legitimate, unless the interpretation is his own.

The story of the Gerasene demoniac is a case in point. It has often been suggested that the reason why Jesus did not enjoin secrecy on this man was that he lived in a Gentile area. Wrede objects that Mark does not say this: 'Why does not the evangelist make it explicitly clear in the text that here we are dealing with a Gentile region?' he asks. In his opinion this story refers to the messianic secret. Jesus said, 'Go and tell your own people' (πρὸς τοὺς σοὺς). Wrede understands this to mean, 'Limit your audience to those who are close to you', and asserts that the man was disobedient in spreading the news throughout the Decapolis.[21] What he seems not to realize is that, if his use of the argument from silence is valid, it can be used against his interpretation just as much as against the interpretation of others. Why, we may ask, does not the evangelist make it explicitly clear that the words 'Go home to your own people and tell them what the Lord has done for you' really mean 'Tell your close family and nobody else'?

This is not the place to evaluate in detail Wrede's use of the argument from silence. Suffice it to say that he uses it extensively, and when Schmidt makes similar extensive use of this argument he is following an established scholarly tradition.

c) *The argument from contradiction*

One of Wrede's main grounds for declaring Mark's narrative to be unhistorical is its supposed inconsistency. Jesus orders people who are healed to keep the fact of their healing secret, but at the same time he frequently performs his miracles in the full glare of publicity. This is described as 'an inner contradiction in Mark's presentation'. Moreover, the prohibitions are pointless because they are disobeyed. Indeed, they produce an opposite effect : 'the more he charged them, the more zealously they proclaimed it' (Mark 7:36).[22] Another problem is the unbelief of the disciples. If they had been witnesses to the prohibitions, and to the messianic acts that provoked them, why did they stumble on the fact of his messiahship so late?[23] And if Jesus told them plainly of his impending death and resurrection, as Mark says he did, why did they still fail to understand?[24] It is clear to Wrede that

> Disciples of the kind presented to us here by Mark are not real figures – disciples who never become any wiser about Jesus after all the wonderful things they see about him – confidants who have no confidence in him and who stand over against him fearfully as before an uncanny enigma and apprehensively discuss his nature among themselves behind his back.[25]

The inconsistencies Wrede alleges here are not logical but psychological – not logically contradictory statements but contraventions of the way in which, in Wrede's opinion, reasonable people could be expected to behave. He seems to think that human behaviour is always rational and predictable, and that the presence of anything enigmatic is a sure sign that the narrative is unhistorical. That Mark should create a narrative full of contradictions is not a problem for Wrede because of his view of the nature of Mark's authorship. Mark was able to juxtapose contradictory ideas, he believes, because he 'simply was not aware of what conclusions for the historical picture must be drawn from each of the two ideas by those reflecting on it.'[26] In other words, the supposedly high incidence of contradiction in Mark's gospel reflects the low intelligence of the author.

Wrede regards Mark's gospel as totally controlled by dogmatic motifs. But he asks the question whether Mark did make at least some attempt to think historically when presenting his dogmatic motifs in historical form. His reply is that Mark did not:

> For a fairly unsophisticated author of antiquity this is, of course, extremely improbable, and in any event Mark does not do it. We saw that he did not establish any connection between the many kinds of prohibition, the different prophecies about death and resurrection and the various expressions of incomprehension on the part of the disciples. In actual fact he did not think through from one point in his presentation to the next.[27]

Because of this lack of sophistication Mark was able to 'inject the dogmatic motif offhandedly into the tale', and was little concerned with how it fitted into its historical context. The 'bad, pointless features' that abound in Mark were there because he was not interested in history. 'They will perhaps be regarded as understandable concomitants of a type of authorship which somewhat gauchely tries to fashion history out of ideas.'[28]

It is significant that Wrede sees Mark's gaucheness (*Unbeholfenheit*) as typical of the age he lived in. It would be most unlikely for 'a fairly unsophisticated author of antiquity' to think historically. We shall discuss in the next chapter the attitude that seems to lie behind a statement of this kind.

d)   *The argument from design*

Wrede uses the argument from design as a further means of casting doubt on the historicity of Mark's statements. According to this argument, any incident that is of dogmatic significance to the author is probably unhistorical. The following are three examples.

(a)   Often in Mark the demons address Jesus in messianic terms. Wrede thinks it quite conceivable in principle that mentally ill people could have done this, and that Mark could have exaggerated the number of cases. But the frequency of this occurrence in Mark and the general statements in 1:34 and 3:11f. show that this point was significant for Mark, and it corresponds to his general view of the relationship between demons and the Son of God. Because of this, the assumption of a historical kernel in the stories ceases to the probable.[29]

(b)   Jülicher and J. Weiss had regarded the saying about parables in Mark 4.11, with certain qualifications, as a genuine saying. But this saying expresses the view of the evangelist. It is therefore incomprehensible to Wrede why the evangelist's view should not be seen as the source of the saying, as of everything else in the passage.[30]

(c)   The passion predictions reflect the belief of the community that Jesus had not only to suffer but to will to suffer. They therefore belong to the category of primitive Christian apologetics.[31] Moreover, the prophecies and their contexts all say the same thing. In other words, they are schematic. This tendency to schematism confirms that 'here we are confronted with the idea of the author or of his time, but not with real history.'[32] One wonders what a modern biographer would think if his or her work were analysed by this criterion – if any attempt to find a recurring pattern in the life of the person under consideration were automatically rejected by the critics on the ground that the pattern must be artificial because the author believed in it.

e)   Conclusion

The four arguments we have considered – from presuppositions, from silence, from contradiction and from design – are all prominent in Schmidt's *Rahmen*. Though Schmidt is dealing with a different aspect of the gospels and his views differ at various points from Wrede's, it is interesting to see how similar is his methodology.

(ii)   Albert Schweitzer

Schweitzer's '*von Reimarus zu Wrede*', known in English as 'The Quest of the Historical Jesus', surveys the researches of German scholars on the life of Jesus up to and including Wrede.[33] Schweitzer agrees with the negative part of Wrede's work – with Wrede's attempt to demonstrate that Mark is full of historical inconsistencies – though he differs radically from Wrede as to the explanation for these inconsistencies. In the course of his book he employs the following arguments.

a)   The argument from consistency

Schweitzer's main presupposition, which he proclaims almost as a dogma, is that there is no place for paradox in biblical scholarship. If a theory is true, it must be consistently and universally true:

Progress always consists in taking one or other of two alternatives, in abandoning the attempt to combine them. The pioneers of progress have therefore always to reckon with the law of mental inertia which manifests itself in the majority – who always go on believing that it is possible to combine that which can no longer be combined, and in fact claim it as a special merit that they, in contrast with the 'one-sided' writers, can do justice to the other side of the question. One must just let them be, till their time is over,and resign oneself not to see the end of it, since it is found by experience that the complete victory of one of two historical alternatives is a matter of two full theological generations.[34]

Schweitzer sees this principle illustrated in three great alternatives between which the study of the life of Jesus has to choose. The first was laid down by Strauss: *either* purely historical *or* purely supernatural. The second was worked out by the Tübingen school and Holtzmann: *either* Synoptic *or* Johannine. The third was laid down by Johannes Weiss and developed by Schweitzer himself: *either* eschatological *or* non-eschatological.[35]

Typical of Schweitzer's approach is his treatment of the phrase 'Son of Man'. He has no use for any interpretation that sees more than one meaning in this phrase. 'Either Jesus used the expression, and used it in a purely Jewish apocalyptic sense, or He did not use it at all.' The authentic Son of Man passages are those in which the expression is used in an apocalyptic sense that goes back to Daniel. Passages where the title does not have this apocalyptic reference 'are to be explained as of literary origin'.[36]

The maintenance of a consistent interpretation is, of course, rendered far easier if all the passages that do not fit in with it can be explained away in this manner. But the question still arises: how can we identify those elements in the multi-faceted tradition of the New Testament that should be consistently upheld? The problem is highlighted by a disagreement between Schweitzer and Wrede, who were both trying to be consistent, but in inconsistent ways. Wrede had argued that all the prohibitions in Mark, both the commands not to publicize the miracles of Jesus and the commands not to reveal his messiahship, must be interpreted in the same way. In Wrede's understanding the miracles of Jesus were seen as proofs of his messiahship, and therefore the two types of prohibition had ultimately the same reference. But in Schweitzer's opinion the miracles were not proofs of messiahship. The idea of the Messiah

as an earthly miracle-worker seemed to him to be at variance with
eschatology, which pictured the Messiah as a heavenly, superterre-
strial being. Therefore, in seeking to carry through a consistently
eschatological view of messiahship, he is forced to reject Wrede's
attempt to carry through a consistently messianic view of the
prohibitions.[37]

What both Wrede and Schweitzer fail to realize is that the teaching
of Jesus was never meant to be consistent in the logical sense of the
term. The only consistent thing about the teaching of Jesus is that
it is consistently paradoxical. The kingdom of God is both present
and future. The secret of the kingdom is both hidden and revealed.
Followers of Jesus must honour their fathers and mothers and hate
their fathers and mothers. Riches must not be accumulated, but
the servant who turns five talents into ten is commended. The road
to eternal life is narrow and few people find it, but people will come
from north, south, east and west into the kingdom of God. The
teaching of Jesus is full of judgment, but he tells us not to judge.
He tells his disciples to buy swords and to put away their swords.
There is no way that the teaching of Jesus can be neatly pigeon-holed
and reduced to one consistent formula. So in practice what scholars
who major in consistency tend to do is to select one element in the
teaching, regard it as normative, and dismiss as secondary accretions
those sayings that seem to reflect a different emphasis.

It is on these grounds that Schmidt takes issue with Schweitzer's
'thoroughgoing eschatology'. He objects that the situation with regard
to the framework of the gospel narratives is too complicated to be
solved so simply. It will not do, he declares, to think one can cure all
the literary, stylistic and textual complications with the standard
prescription of a set theory, without engaging in any investigation of
individual passages.[38] This is well said, and shows that Schmidt was
well aware of the limitations of the quest for consistency; and yet, in
a sense, his whole book exemplifies Schweitzer's approach. He begins
by stating his presuppositions as to how the gospel was composed,
and then tries to make every passage in the gospels conform to those
presuppositions. The examples of forced exegesis that abound in
Schmidt's book are the fruit of this Procrustean approach. His 'set
theory' is different from Schweitzer's, but his methodology is very
similar.

There is an interesting section in Schweitzer's discussion of D.F.
Strauss that illustrates the ambiguities of the quest for consistency.

Schweitzer relates how, in the third edition of his *Life of Jesus*, Strauss
made some amazing concessions. He confessed to some hesitation
about his former doubts concerning the genuineness and credibility
of the Fourth Gospel, and said that the historic personality of Jesus
had begun again to take on intelligible outlines for him. In the fourth
edition he withdrew these hesitations, and confessed that he did not
know how he could have vacillated in his opinions. Schweitzer gives
a psychological explanation for this episode, and explains that Strauss
had suffered more than people realized from the hostility of his
enemies and longed for peace.[39] The explanation is convincing: life is
full of similar examples of inconsistent behaviour. Yet a few pages
later Schweitzer quotes Strauss's assertion that a similar inconsistency
on the part of John the Baptist cannot be historical:

> In the narrative of the baptism we may take it as certainly unhistorical
> that the Baptist received a revelation of the Messianic dignity of Jesus,
> otherwise he could not later have come to doubt this.[40]

The idea that John the Baptist, under the psychological pressures of
imprisonment, could have come to doubt his earlier experience is
adjudged by Strauss to be 'certainly unhistorical'. How little do such
armchair judgments correspond to the ambiguities of life as it is
actually lived.

b) *The argument from presuppositions*

Like Wrede, Schweitzer accepts the presuppositions of rationalism,
which he believes to have become established dogma since the
publication of D.F. Strauss's 'Life of Jesus'. According to
Schweitzer, Strauss laid down two alternatives between which the
study of the life of Jesus had to choose: *either* purely historical *or* purely
supernatural.[41] In opting for the former alternative Strauss's book was
'the work which made an end of miracle as a matter of historical belief,
and gave the mythological explanation its due.'[42] What the adoption
of the 'purely historical' point of view means in practice can be
illustrated from Schweitzer's treatment of the passion predictions.
Pfleiderer and Wrede were right, he asserts, to treat these predictions
as historically inexplicable, because 'the necessity of Jesus' death . . .
is not a necessity which arises out of the historical course of events.
There was not present any natural ground for such a resolve on the
part of Jesus.'[43] Schweitzer sees the attitude of Jesus as rooted in his
eschatological beliefs; but his view makes no more allowance than the

view of Pfleiderer and Wrede for prophetic inspiration in the normally accepted understanding of that phrase as a gift from God.

Schweitzer also shares Schmidt's presupposition that the gospel writers were artless and unsophisticated. He describes the evangelists as 'simple Christians without literary gift'. He sees this as an advantage for our modern study of the life of Jesus: whereas our picture of Socrates comes to us from literary men who exercised their creative ability on the portrait, the gospel writers simply reproduced the material available.[44]

They were thus very different from the German scholars whose work Schweitzer is analysing. Schweitzer begins his book with a eulogy of German theology as a product of the German temperament, and particularly of German research into the life of Jesus, which he describes as 'the most tremendous thing which the religious consciousness has ever dared or done'.[45] One gets the impression that for Schweitzer the interpretation of the life, death and resurrection of Jesus by the early disciples as recorded in the New Testament was of less significance than the reinterpretation of these events by German scholars in the nineteenth century. The contribution of the early Christians was to reproduce material they did not understand. The task of understanding was undertaken by German scholars, though Schweitzer admits that that task was still only at a preliminary stage.[46]

c) *The argument from silence*

Schweitzer believes that according to Mark's gospel the ministry of Jesus lasted for less than one year, since Mark mentions only one passover. He calls this 'something quite incomprehensible' in the light of all the things that have to be crammed into that one year.[47] The assumption lying behind this statement is that, had the evangelists believed the ministry of Jesus to have covered more than one passover, they would have been bound to mention this – in other words, that their aim was to be comprehensive in their coverage. This assumption is clearly expressed in Schweitzer's comment on the order and inner connection of the events in the life of Jesus:

> If the tradition preserved by the Synoptists really includes all that happened during the time that Jesus was with His disciples, the attempt to discover the connexion must succeed sooner or later. It becomes more and more clear that this presupposition is indispensable to the investigation. If it is merely a fortuitous series of episodes that the

Evangelists have handed down to us, we may give up the attempt to arrive at a critical reconstruction of the life of Jesus as hopeless.[48]

Schweitzer here presents two possibilities: either the evangelists presented a fortuitous series of episodes, or they presented a comprehensive coverage of the life of Jesus. There are, however, other possibilities between these two extremes. They could have aimed to give a representative sample of the various activities of Jesus, with each recorded event representing numerous similar unrecorded events. They could have presented a historical outline that was correct as far as it went, but included long gaps of many months' duration that they were unable to cover through lack of space. On Schweitzer's assumption that they aimed to provide comprehensive coverage, Mark's reference to only one passover in the ministry of Jesus must mean that he thought there only was one. But the sole evidence Schweitzer adduces for his assumption is the difficulties modern chronologists would face without it.

Schweitzer, like Wrede, employs the argument from silence to suggest that Jesus did not think of himself as a teacher. He asks the question: 'If all the controversial discourses and sayings and answers to questions, which were so to speak wrung from Him, were subtracted from the sum of His utterances, how much of a didactic preaching of Jesus would be left over?'[49] Such a statistical use of the argument from silence rests on a misunderstanding of the nature of the synoptic record, in which virtually every kind of activity in which Jesus engaged is represented only by a few paradigmatic examples.

A good example of Schweitzer's use of the argument from silence is his treatment of the triumphal entry. He asks four questions: How did the entry come about? Why did the Roman soldiers do nothing about it? Why was it completely ignored in the subsequent controversies, as if it had never taken place? And why was it not brought up at the trial of Jesus?[50] In the light of these questions he propounds the strange theory that Jesus planned his entry to be messianic, in fulfilment of Zechariah 9:9, but none of the crowd realized this. Thus the entry was 'Messianic for Jesus, but not Messianic for the people'[51]

The difficulties Schweitzer feels about this story are products of the argument from silence. His question as to why the triumphal entry was completely ignored in the subsequent narrative makes sense only if we accept his theory that the evangelists aimed to provide comprehensive coverage. But this was clearly not their aim. According to Mark 14:56 many people bore witness against Jesus when he appeared before the Sanhedrin, but Mark does not specify what these people said, whether they referred to the triumphal entry or whether they did not. Given the highly condensed nature of Mark's narrative (including the passion narrative) it is impossible to discover any significance in silences of this sort.

iii)   Julius Wellhausen[52]

In his 'Introduction to the first three gospels', published in 1905, Wellhausen summarizes the significant features of Mark.[53] In the main he concentrates on Mark's deficiencies and employs the following arguments to highlight these deficiencies.

a)   *The argument from presuppositions*

Underlying the whole of Wellhausen's presentation is the theory of Markan artlessness. In Wellhausen's opinion the material in Mark (as in the other synoptic gospels) is put together loosely and artlessly (*lose und ohne Kunst*).[54] He thinks of Mark primarily as a redactor, who took what was offered him by the tradition. Much of this tradition was not apostolic in origin but had a somewhat crudely popular nature. This appears particularly in the accounts of miracles and of the recognition of Jesus by demons. Wellhausen cannot imagine a genuine eyewitness such as Peter telling such stories. Rather, they are characteristic of popular taste.[55]

In concentrating on the miracle stories as evidence for the 'crudely popular' nature of Mark and his sources, Wellhausen presupposes the same rationalist dogma as Wrede. He asks rhetorically: could Peter have told the stories of Jesus walking on the water, of demons moving into pigs or of dumb and blind people being healed with spittle? He assumes the answer must be 'no', presumably on the basis that these stories, known to be unhistorical on rationalist grounds, cannot go back to eyewitness evidence.

b)   *The argument from design*

Wellhausen accuses Mark of deliberately emphasizing certain things and understating others. For example, he argues that the charge of blasphemy at the trial of Jesus must have related not to the messiahship of Jesus (as suggested by 14:61–64) but to the blasphemy against the temple referred to in 14:58. In his opinion Mark has pushed the temple blasphemy into the background, because the early Christian church in Jerusalem had reasons for wanting to do this. The high-handed action of Jesus in cleansing the temple (11:15–19) has been similarly pushed into the background. The temple cleansing clearly triggered the intervention of the chief priests (11:27ff.), but this is obscured in Mark's account by the insertion of the second part of the fig tree story (11:20–25). The flight of the disciples (14:50) has been 'pushed to one side'; and the statement in 16:7 that Jesus had promised to meet his disciples in Galilee is regarded as an attempt to justify that flight – the disciples were not running away but making a planned tactical withdrawal to Galilee in obedience to Jesus's command.[56]

Wellhausen comments that Mark, when revising his material, did not wipe out the original elements. In other words, he does not accuse Mark of suppressing the facts, but of not emphasizing some of them to the requisite degree. With the help of his creative imagination Wellhausen seems to believe he can discern not only the facts but also their relative importance, and read Mark's mind as to the motives that led him to assign to these facts a different priority. One wonders how the work of any historian, ancient or modern, could stand up to this kind of subjective critical judgment regarding the relative importance of a series of facts.

c) *The argument from textual tradition*

I have noted only one example of Wellhausen's use of this argument, but it is so striking, and anticipates Schmidt's use of the same argument so closely, that it is worthy of mention. Wellhausen is castigating Mark for the scantiness of his material. He points out that Mark includes few personal names and 'even Jairus is not named in D.'[57] The omission of Jairus' name by Codex D and a few Latin manuscripts in Mark 5:22 is not thought to be of any significance by most commentators. D (Codex Bezae) is a manuscript of notorious eccentricity. Wellhausen mentions this particular variant (without suggesting that it represents Mark's original text) because it illustrates what seems to him to be a Markan characteristic. This kind of selective use of textual variants (particularly those of D) to reinforce an argument is a feature we have already observed in Schmidt's *Rahmen*.

d) *The argument from contradiction*

According to Wellhausen, Mark's version of the parable of the mustard seed betrays its late provenance by the 'Matthaean' reference to the kingdom of God, which does not appear elsewhere in Mark in the same form.[58] It is interesting that a few pages earlier Wellhausen has commented on the scantiness of the material in Mark.[59] But even within this scanty material he does not seem to think it possible that a phrase occurring in one parable can be genuine unless it occurs in other parables also. The fact that the phrase occurs in a similar context more frequently in Matthew is apparently taken to mean that Matthew has invented it, and that therefore it cannot be authentic in its one occurrence in Mark.

The parable of the vineyard and its tenants (12:1–12) is also deemed inauthentic on the grounds that its open hostility to the Jewish leaders is inconsistent with the cautious and evasive way in which Jesus treats them elsewhere.[60] The idea that the attitude of Jesus could have changed as the prospect of his death drew closer is not taken seriously – Jesus must be totally consistent throughout his ministry.

In one passage Wellhausen's use of the argument from contradiction strikingly anticipates the use of this argument by Schmidt. As Schmidt so often does, he takes a Greek word absolutely literally, and then on the basis of this literal interpretation accuses Mark of blatant inconsistency. The passage in question is Wellhausen's comment on Mark 1:16–34.[61]

In these verses are recorded (i) the call of the four fishermen (vv. 16–20); (ii) an exorcism in the synagogue (vv. 21–28); (iii) the healing of Peter's mother-in-law (vv. 29–31); (iv) other healings in the evening (vv. 32–34). Wellhausen pours scorn on Mark for crowding all these events into one day – and a sabbath day at that, when the fishermen would not be working. But what are the grounds for this scorn? Verse 21 reads: καὶ εἰσπορεύονται εἰς Καφαρναούμ. καὶ εὐθὺς τοῖς σάββασιν εἰσελθὼν εἰς τὴν συναγωγὴν ἐδίδασκεν. (And they entered Capernaum. And immediately on the Sabbath day he entered the synagogue and began to teach). Wellhausen takes the word εὐθύς (immediately) in the most literally possible way.[62] As soon as Jesus entered Capernaum, presumably without stopping for a meal or a wash, he immediately entered the synagogue and immediately,without waiting to pray or to worship, began to teach. Only by such a literal interpretation of the word εὐθύς can one reach the conclusion that the call of the disciples occurred on the same day as the visit to the synagogue. Such literalism was far from Mark's mind. It is more natural to translate, with the Good News Bible, 'and on the next Sabbath Jesus went to the synagogue and began to teach'.

e) *The argument from silence*

The argument from silence is Wellhausen's favourite argument. In his long catalogue of Mark's deficiencies it is Mark's failure to include items he should have included that recurs again and again. He complains that Mark records only comparatively few events in the Galilee ministry. There are few personal names, and the disciples are mere window-dressing (*Staffage*). We are not told how Jesus lived, ate and drank or associated with his companions. We are told he taught in the synagogue, but not what he taught. The ordinary is omitted, only the extraordinary is reported. This can only partially be explained on the grounds that these things were already known to Mark's readers. Wellhausen concludes: 'the scantiness of the tradition is still striking.'[63]

He detects the same scantiness in the Passion Narrative. The reason for Judas' betrayal is mysterious. Various people appear on the scene without any preparation, e.g. the provider of the upper room, the anointing woman, the youth who fled naked, Joseph of Arimathaea and the group of ministering women. Even the fact that the crucifixion took place on a Friday is only mentioned in a kind of parenthesis.[64]

Throughout Mark's gospel, Wellhausen believes, the marks of history are missing. There is no chronology, no firm date. The events described are unmotivated and not practically connected. Geographical details are vague (e.g. 'in a house'), there is no itinerary, and the isolated anecdotes are not sufficient for a biography of Jesus. There is no evidence of any attempt by those who ate and drank with Jesus to convey to others his personality. There are some personal features (e.g. Jesus' knowledge of people and his compassion), but the miracles are valued mainly as signs of his messianic power. For Wellhausen the lack of detail about the everyday life that Jesus shared with his disciples is one of the decisive indications that Mark's tradition was not apostolic.[65]

In appraising Mark in this way Wellhausen writes unashamedly from a twentieth-century point of view. He writes: 'We should not exclude the Passion Narrative from the judgment that in Mark's gospel on the whole the marks of history are missing. Our thirst for knowledge remains unsatisfied.'[66] It is Mark's failure to satisfy 'our thirst for knowledge' – to answer the kind of questions we in the twentieth century are asking – that shows him not to be a proper historian. Wellhausen's approach to history is dominated by the importance of 'facts' – names, dates etc. It reflects a Western culture in which it is possible, on a British TV programme, for a person to be given the title 'Mastermind' by virtue of providing a series of answers to questions, each one of which can immediately be labelled 'correct' or 'incorrect'. When one studies the question and answer sessions in which Jesus was involved, very few of his statements can be labelled 'correct' in the modern sense of that term. Our obsession with 'facts' should be seen as a peculiarity of the twentieth century rather than as a standard by which other cultures should be judged.

The contrast between the way Mark wrote and Wellhausen's conception of the way history should be written is similar in some respects to the contrast between the plays of William Shakespeare and those of George Bernard Shaw. Shaw's play, *The Man of Destiny*, is prefaced by five pages of introduction, including an outline of Napoleon's career up to that point and detailed descriptions of the inn at which the action takes place, of the innkeeper and of Napoleon himself. Shakespeare's plays contain nothing of this sort. The various characters make their entrances without introduction or explanation. No doubt this contrast can be explained in part by the changes in the theatrical world over three hundred years – by the fact, for example, that scenery and props were rudimentary in Shakespeare's day and elaborate in Shaw's. But there is also a difference of approach. Shakespeare allows the personality of his characters to emerge gradually from what they do or say; for Shaw everything has to be explained first and then illustrated. Basically, Wellhausen is saying that Mark should have written in the style of Shaw rather than in that of Shakespeare.

iv) The Framework of the Gospel Narrative

As already stated, Schmidt's debt to his predecessors lies largely in the area of methodology. But there is also a debt in respect of content.

When the three scholars we have been considering touch on the question of the Markan framework, they do so in terms very similar to Schmidt's.

In Wrede's opinion there is no internal sequence in Mark. There are the odd cross-references to earlier material such as 6:52 and 8:17ff., but on the whole the gospel consists of isolated stories placed side by side. Mark does indeed connect the stories, but it is a connection of ideas, not of historical development. Mark is presenting dogmatic ideas such as the Messianic Secret in a historical guise. In doing so he does not think through from one point in his presentation to the next, and there is therefore no logical connection between the various events related.[67]

Schweitzer puts forward a broadly similar view. He rejects the approach of so many nineteenth-century 'Lives of Jesus', that sees the psychological development of Jesus as the key to the gospel narrative. He insists that Mark knew nothing of any development in Jesus or any conflict in his mind between different conceptions of messiahship. The death knell of such ideas has been sounded by the thoroughgoing scepticism of Wrede and the thoroughgoing eschatological approach of Johannes Weiss and Schweitzer himself. As a result of these two approaches we must now dispense with the connecting links between the various pericopes, look at each pericope separately and recognize that it is difficult to pass from one to the other. It is no longer possible to travel straight through the gospels as if one were on an express train, using a psychological theory to bind all the units together. That ticket office is now closed. There is a station at the end of each unit and connections are not guaranteed. Not only is there no obvious connection between the units; in almost every case there is a positive break in the connection. And there is a great deal in the Markan narrative that is inexplicable and even self-contradictory.[68]

Schweitzer thus sees Mark's Gospel as a collection of unconnected or improperly connected fragments, with no common thread of logic or psychology. When Schmidt quotes Schweitzer's opinion in the introduction to his book, he rejects Schweitzer's thoroughgoing eschatology, but is clearly in substantial agreement with his analysis of the nature of the Gospel.[69]

Wellhausen regards Mark mainly as a redactor, who took over what the tradition offered him. Mark's editorial work consisted in arranging the material in three sections and adding introductions, conclusions, transitions, summaries and (in the case of floating sayings) audience specifications. So far as the tradition is concerned, Wellhausen does not have a high opinion of it. Very little of it goes back to the apostles. For one thing, it is strong with regard to Jerusalem but weak with regard to Galilee. For another, it is full of miraculous elements that reflect popular taste and had propaganda value in early Christian evangelism. The lack of information about the everyday intercourse of Jesus with his disciples suggests that the tradition does not go back to the apostles. The bulk of the material has a somewhat coarsely popular nature, as a result of a long period of oral transmission. Wellhausen's interest is in the pre-Markan tradition, and in this respect he anticipates the later work of the form critics. Mark is for him simply a redactor.[70]

These three approaches share certain common factors, which Schmidt was able to take over and treat as presuppositions. Mark is seen basically as a redactor, who has loosely combined isolated units of tradition without providing a common thread of either history or psychology. Mark is not seen as a creative artist. When Wrede describes the Gospel of Mark as belonging to the history of dogma,[71] he is not attributing to Mark the creative ability of a theologian. He believes that the dogmatic element in Mark (particularly the idea of the Messianic Secret) was not invented by Mark but taken by him from the tradition and juxtaposed with other contradictory elements in an illogical jumble.[72] All three scholars, despite their different approaches, see Mark as an anthology of contradictions. Whether the various elements are regarded as dogmatic (Wrede), eschatological (Schweitzer) or coarsely popular (Wellhausen), Mark's value is seen to lie in his faithful reproduction of these elements, without attempting (or having the ability) to reduce them all to a coherent whole. Schmidt took over this point of view from his predecessors, and it became a presupposition of his own work.

Notes

1 William Wrede, *The Messianic Secret in the Gospels* tr. J.C.G. Greig (James Clarke, Cambridge and London 1971), hereafter referred to as (E). William Wrede, *Das Messiasgeheimnis in den Evangelien* (Vandenhoeck and Ruprecht, Gottingen 1901, 1963³), hereafter referred to as (G). Quotations are almost all from the English translation, with occasional direct translation from the German original.
2 Ibid. 129 (E), 129 (G)
3 Ibid. 228 (E), 227 (G): 'Thus hardly any possibility remains other than the

suggestion that the idea of the secret arose at a time when as yet there was no knowledge of any messianic claim on the part of Jesus on earth.' Cf. 230 (E), 229 (G): 'What I have just been saying should be regarded as a tentative solution (*Versuch*).'

4   Christopher Tuckett (ed) *The Messianic Secret* (Fortress Press, Philadelphia and SPCK, London 1983) 1.

5   Wrede, *Secret* 9(E), 7(G)

6   Ibid. 50 (E), 48 (G)

7   Ibid. 27 (E), 26 (G)

8   Ibid. 103 (E), 104 (G)

9   Ibid. 53 (E), 51 (G)

10 Ibid. 87 (E), 87 (G)

11 Charles Staples Lewis, *Christian Reflections* (Collins, Glasgow 1981) 198. Lewis discussed the question of miracles in more detail in his book *Miracles* (Collins, London 1960).

12 Wrede, *Secret* 143 (E), 143 (G)

13 Ibid. 15 (E), 14 (G)

14 Ibid. 143 (E) 142f. (G)

15 Ibid. 15f. (E), 14 (G)

16 Ibid. 141ff. (E), 141f. (G)

17 Ibid. 20 (E), 18 (G). One wonders what kind of comment Wrede would have liked Mark (or Jesus) to make. Perhaps, in Wrede's emended version, the words of Jesus in Mark 2:10 might read: 'I want you to know that the Son of Man has authority on earth to forgive sins, and that I am using the phrase "Son of Man" in an enigmatic sense.' Or alternatively, Mark 2:12 might read: 'They were all amazed and praised God, saying, "We have never seen anything like this! And we do not understand what he means by the phrase 'Son of Man'." ' The sense of anticlimax that such additions would bring to Mark's narrative would not worry Wrede, since he, like Schmidt, constantly criticizes Mark from a logical rather than a literary point of view.

18 Ibid. 45 (E), 43 (G)

19 Ibid. 44 (E), 42 (G)

20 Ibid. 119 (E), 119 (G)

21 Ibid. 140f. (E), 140f. (G)

22 Ibid. 18f. (E), 16ff. (G)

23 Ibid. 37f. (E), 36 (G)

24 Ibid. 56f. (E), 54f. (G)

25 Ibid. 103 (E), 104 (G). On the question of the 'illogical' behaviour of the disciples see further *Seven Pillories* 116–119.

26 Wrede, *Secret* 128 (E), 128 (G)

27 Ibid. 132 (E), 132 (G)

28 Ibid. 135 (E), 135 (G)

29 Ibid. 32f. (E), 30f. (G)

30 Ibid. 63f. (E), 61 (G)

31 Ibid. 88ff. (E), 89f. (G)

32 Ibid. 100 (E), 101 (G)

33 Albert Schweitzer, *The Quest of the Historical Jesus*, tr. W. Montgomery (Black, London, 1954[3]).

34 Ibid. 237f.

35   Ibid. 237.
36   Ibid. 281f.
37   Ibid. 345f.
38   Schmidt, *Rahmen* VIIIf.
39   Schweitzer, *Quest* 72.
40   Ibid. 81.
41   Ibid. 237.
42   Ibid. 95.
43   Ibid. 384f.
44   Ibid. 6.
45   Ibid. 1f.
46   Ibid. 398.
47   Ibid. 350.
48   Ibid. 7.
49   Ibid. 351.
50   Ibid. 332. In support of the application of the argument from silence to this
     passage, Schweitzer quotes a comment of William Wrede: 'The Messianic
     acclamation at the entry into Jerusalem is in Mark quite an isolated incident. It
     has no sequel, neither is there any preparation for it beforehand.'
51   Ibid. 391f.
52   Julius Wellhausen spent much of his life as a professor of Old Testament and of
     Semitic languages, and turned to the analysis of the Gospels towards the end of
     his career. A fascinating critique of his *Prolegomena to the History of Israel* is to be
     found in Herman Wouk, *This is my God* (Collins, London 1959) 287–93. Wouk
     is both a distinguished author and an observant Jew. He claims to have checked
     in the Hebrew Old Testament every textual reference in the *Prolegomena* – a feat
     which, as he says, will probably never be accomplished again. While his criticism
     is limited to Wellhausen's work on the Old Testament, his analysis of Well-
     hausen's methodology has a more general relevance – in particular, in showing
     how 'literary analysis is not a scientific method'.
53   Julius Wellhausen, *Einleitung in die drei ersten Evangelien* (Georg Reiner, Berlin
     1905) 43–57.
54   Ibid. 15.
55   Ibid. 53.
56   Ibid. 50.
57   Ibid. 47. The omission of Jairus' name in D is mentioned as an ancillary fact in
     Schmidt's discussion (147) of the 'problem' of Jairus being referred to in
     different ways. See above p. 48n.18.
58   Ibid. 55.
59   Ibid. 47.
60   Ibid. 55.
61   Ibid. 46f.
62   It was recognized in Wellhausen's day that the literal meaning of εὐθύς could
     not be pressed in Mark. Wellhausen's contemporary H.B. Swete noted that in
     the Septuagint καὶ εὐθύς is used to translate the Hebrew "w'hinneh" (and
     behold) (H.B. Swete, *The Gospel according to St. Mark* (Macmillan, London
     1898) 8, commenting on Mark 1:10). More recently P. Ellingworth has argued
     that εὐθύς in Mark often does not mean 'immediately' and may not even be an

expression of time at all (Paul Ellingworth, 'How soon is "immediately" in Mark?' *The Bible Translator* Vol. 29 No. 4 October 1978 pp. 414–419).

63 Wellhausen, *Einleitung* 47.
64 Ibid. 50f.
65 Ibid. 51–3.
66 Ibid. 51.
67 Wrede, *Secret* 132 (E), 131f. (G).
68 Schweitzer, *Quest* 330–2.
69 Schmidt, *Rahmen* VII – IX.
70 Wellhausen, *Einleitung* 53.
71 Wrede, *Secret* 131 (E), 131 (G).
72 Ibid. 145 (E), 145 (G): 'Is the idea of a messianic secret an invention of Mark's? That is a quite impossible notion. . . . Historically speaking, the idea cannot be understood as coming directly from Mark. We find it there ready-made, and Mark is under its sway, so that we cannot even speak of a *Tendenz*.' As Christopher Tuckett points out (*Secret 12*), it was Bultmann who popularized the view that the secrecy theory was a Markan invention.

Part IV

15

Schmidt's Influence on Later Scholarship

Before we consider Schmidt's influence on twentieth century scholarship, we should note the fact that two aspects of his thesis have not
found favour with later scholars. The first is his theory of travelling
introductions. Schmidt, as we have seen, carefully divided the introductory material in Mark into two categories: introductory formulae
taken over from the tradition and extra details added by Mark.
Subsequent scholarship has ignored the former category and attributed almost all such material to Mark. Typical is the comment of
Rudolf Bultmann:

> The first step is to distinguish between the traditional material which
> the evangelists used and their editorial additions. This task, which
> Wellhausen recognized, was systematically carried through by K.L.
> Schmidt. . . . It may be seen quite clearly that the original tradition was
> made up almost entirely of brief single units (sayings or short narra-
> tives), and that almost all references to time and place which serve to
> connect up the single sections into a larger context are the editorial
> work of the evangelists.[1]

Here all Schmidt's painstaking attempts to distinguish between
time/place statements which travelled around with the stories and
time/place statements added by Mark are simply ignored. Only the
Markan additions are regarded as significant.

One can understand why this aspect of Schmidt's work has not
found favour with other scholars. The early form critics regarded the
gospel pericopes as pure stories, not as stories in a framework. Redaction critics, from Marxsen onwards, have recognized Mark's literary
ability, and this has made it more natural for them to think of the
Markan framework in terms of creative artistry than in terms of blind
copying. As for modern holistic approaches to Mark, they will naturally
not be sympathetic to a theory that is essentially disintegrative. For

example, in his commentary on Mark 8:1, Schmidt attributes the words ἐν ἐκείναις ταῖς ἡμέραις (in those days) to the tradition, and the word πάλιν (again) to Mark.[2] This scissors-and-paste approach to literary criticism is rightly discredited. As W.R. Telford says:

> In the case of Mark, the selection and arrangement of material and overall composition may provide a better clue to the evangelist's intention than the alterations he is deemed to have made in his source material. Attention has been drawn to the limitations of a purely (German) tradition-redaction approach, with its meticulous division of the text into verses and fractions of verses allocated either to the evangelist or his sources.[3]

The theory of travelling introductions richly deserves the oblivion to which later scholarship has assigned it. At the same time, it is important to recognize how important a part this theory played in Schmidt's overall thesis. In opposing Wendling's view that Mark was dependent on written sources, Schmidt writes: 'Anyone who, like me, lays the major emphasis on the existence of isolated pericopes along with their introductory or framework elements is bound to make a different analysis.'[4] In other words, the existence in the tradition of pericopes with framework elements that were as rigidly fixed as any written source makes the hypothesis of actual written sources unnecessary. Elsewhere he describes these framework elements as embellishments that have coiled themselves like a creeper around the stories to which they belong (*ein reiches Rankenwerk von chronologischen und topographischen Angaben ist vorhanden, das sich um die einzelnen Erzählungen geschlungen hat*).[5] This raises the question: can one tear away the creeper and attempt to uncover the pure stories underneath without causing structural damage to the whole theory?

The second aspect of Schmidt's work that has fallen out of favour is his estimate of Mark's literary ability. As we have seen, Schmidt has a low opinion of Mark not only as a historian but also as an artist. He uses terms such as 'clumsy' and 'artless' to describe Mark's work. Subsequent critics, particularly in the latter half of the twentieth century, have not endorsed this judgment, and honour Mark as a skilful craftsman. Telford concludes his summary of the last thirty years of Markan study as follows:

> We began this survey by noting a traditional view that Mark's Gospel was unsophisticated and untheological. The literary explosion to which it has given rise, however, in the last thirty years has surely chronicled the reversal of this judgment.[6]

At the same time Telford, like most modern scholars, regards Schmidt's main thesis as proven.[7] Presumably Schmidt's low estimate of Mark's literary ability is seen as a minor blemish in his presentation that does not invalidate his core argument. But is this in fact the case? Schmidt's thesis is that Mark composed the framework of his gospel by taking over introductory material word for word from his sources and adding extra words here and there as best he could. This scissors-and-paste approach is basic to Schmidt's argument, and to be believable requires Mark to be an unintelligent redactor. More-over, many of Schmidt's supporting arguments depend for their validity on a low estimate of Mark's ability. In his use of the *argument from silence*, Schmidt never asks whether Mark's omission of corroborative detail could be due to literary considerations; Mark's silence is consistently attributed either to his own ignorance or to that of his sources. In his use of the *argument from contradiction*, Schmidt assumes that Mark, like the other evangelists, recorded mutually inconsistent statements without having the intelligence to realize their inconsistency. His use of the *argument from literary criticism* consists of the application of logical criteria without any feel for the gospels as literature or for their authors as literary artists. It seems obvious that these methodological deficiencies must affect our estimate of Schmidt's work as a whole. There is a logical inconsistency in alleging, as many scholars today seem to do, that Schmidt's basic thesis is proven and has rightly become part of modern critical orthodoxy, while at the same time rejecting the evaluation of Mark as a clumsy redactor on which that thesis depends from start to finish.

The way in which our estimate of Mark as a person affects our estimate of his compositional technique is highlighted by Martin Hengel:

> The Gospel was written for the audience to listen to, and therefore is anything but an artificial literary composition written at a desk, stuck together from obscure written sources, countless notes and flysheets. Here we should not simply project our own extracts and notes, our relatively mechanical 'scientific' ways of working on to Mark. Behind this work there is neither a mere collector of amorphous popular 'community tradition' (how are we to imagine that) somewhere in the Gentile Christian churches, nor an anonymous, poetically inspired, Gentile Christian man of letters, but a theological teacher who himself must have been a master of the word and an authority in early Christianity. A Mr. Nobody would hardly have undertaken the revolutionary innovation of writing a gospel.[8]

In one respect Schmidt has indeed made out his case. He exposes the futility of the attempt by some earlier scholars to provide a firm chronological sequence for all the events in the gospels. Schmidt shows conclusively that the gospels do not provide the data necessary for such an attempt, nor do they intend to do so. But Schmidt's quarrel is not only with the conservative nineteenth-century authors of 'Lives of Jesus'; it is also with scholars such as Wellhausen and Johannes Weiss whose views were more radical but who nevertheless assigned a measure of historical value to the Markan framework. In opposing these scholars, Schmidt seeks to show that, for example, the references to Capernaum in 2:1 or to six days in 9:2 are just as unreliable as vague references to 'a house' or to 'those days'. His contention is that, with the exception of the passion narrative, the Markan framework as a whole is historically valueless.

In his book 'A New Quest of the Historical Jesus' published forty years after *Rahmen* in 1959, J.M. Robinson indicated that by that time Schmidt's thesis had already become orthodox dogma for New Testament scholarship. He pointed out that the old quest of the historical Jesus had been brought to an end, not by form criticism, but by the scholars who laid the foundation for form criticism. In his observation, the mention of 'forms' in scholarly discussion of gospel passages had already to a large extent passed out of vogue, even in Germany; but the basic orientation with regard to the Gospels, of which form criticism was but one manifestation, still continued as the basis of scholarship. This basic orientation was the axiom that *all* the tradition about Jesus survived only in so far as it served some function in the life and worship of the primitive church.

Robinson identified Wellhausen, Wrede and Schmidt as the key figures in promoting this approach. Wellhausen's distinction between the historical reality of the life of Jesus and the church's use of it in worship had been carried forward by the detailed analysis of Wrede and Schmidt. Wrede had 'demonstrated' that Mark was not a historian but a theologian. Schmidt had 'demonstrated' that the order of events in the gospels was largely topical or theological, without any serious interest in chronology or geography. Robinson concluded:

> The basic theses of these works have not been disproved, and therefore must continue to be presupposed in current scholarship conversant with them.[9]

Robinson here treats Schmidt not as a form critic but as a precursor of form criticism. Chronologically, Schmidt's book was contemporary with the great form-critical works of Dibelius and Bultmann, and he is often referred to as a form critic.[10] But logically, as Robinson rightly observes, his book is related to the viewpoint of the previous generation. He limits his investigation to the framework of the gospel narrative and does not consider in detail the individual stories, let alone classifying their forms. While he is emphatic in setting the context of these stories within the worshipping community, he does not explore this idea in detail, but takes it over from scholars such as Wellhausen who preceded him.[11]

His distinctive contribution is the separation of story from framework: the attempt to demonstrate that the stories in Mark originally circulated in isolation without any context, and that the Markan framework has no historical basis.[12] This theory provides a logical base for the form-critical classification of the stories according to their role in the life of the community; it also provides a logical base for the redaction-critical view that the framework represents the creative theology of the evangelist. Redaction critics assess Mark's editorial work more highly than Schmidt, but they presuppose the same separation between tradition and redaction that he does.[13] It is also arguable that Schmidt's thesis provides a logical base for the 'flight from history' of modern holistic approaches to Mark. If Mark has taken over a community tradition several times removed from the original eyewitnesses and provided it with an almost totally unhistorical framework, as Schmidt asserts, one can understand why any attempt to interpret Mark from a historical point of view should be thought to be meaningless.[14] Schmidt's thesis has provided a foundation not just for form criticism but for much else besides.

The main question raised by Robinson's analysis, however, is whether we should continue to presuppose Schmidt's thesis for the foreseeable future. In considering this question, it may be helpful to divide Schmidt's presentation into two elements: its dogmatic core and its supporting arguments. The dogmatic core consists of his basic presupposition: Mark's total dependence on early church storytellers, whose stories were all told out of context. Schmidt succeeds in showing that it is possible to interpret the evidence of the gospels in a way that is consistent with his presupposition. But this does not prove that his presupposition is valid.[15] In a court of law counsels for the prosecution and for the defence are often able to interpret the same evidence in the interests of two diametrically opposed points of view. In such cases the jury has to decide between these two points of view in the light of all the arguments presented. The same is true of Schmidt's thesis. The key question is whether his supporting arguments are convincing enough to validate the presupposition in whose interest they are presented.

We must therefore, in order to evaluate Schmidt's thesis, ask five basic questions. Is it valid to use the *argument from design* in the way Schmidt uses it, and argue that if any statement fits in with Mark's overall plan, Mark must have invented it? Is it valid to use the *argument from silence* in the way Schmidt uses it, and argue that the absence from Mark of features we should expect in a twentieth-century biography means that he was incapable of thinking historically? Is it valid to use the *argument from contradiction* in the way Schmidt uses it – to raise a series of pedantic quibbles and argue that Mark was too stupid to realize the resultant inconsistencies? Is it valid to use the *argument from textual tradition* in the way Schmidt uses it – to regard the alterations made by Marcion or by scribes copying out gospel manuscripts as evidence for what the evangelists must also have done? Is it valid to use the *argument from literary criticism* in the way Schmidt uses it – to follow set criteria about the use of language instead of trying to understand Mark as a creative and intelligent author? If we think Schmidt's techniques are valid, we shall accord a high degree of probability to his conclusions. But if his techniques are invalid, we are bound to regard with suspicion the conclusions reached by the use of these techniques.

The perception that many of Schmidt's arguments are unsound does not, of course, prove that his thesis is incorrect. It would be logically possible for a thesis propounded on the basis of a series of unsound arguments to turn out nevertheless to be correct, though for quite different reasons. What militates against Schmidt's thesis is not only the weakness of the arguments in its favour but also its inherent improbability. He paints a picture of the early Christian communities that strains our credulity to breaking-point.

Schmidt and his followers ask us to believe the following picture. Mark wrote his gospel some forty years after the events he describes, at a time when hundreds of eyewitnesses of the ministry of Jesus were still alive. He did not consult any of these eyewitnesses, nor had he ever had contact with them earlier in his life, but relied exclusively on stories that were circulating in the church to which he belonged. The gospel we know as Mark's gospel was published either anonymously or under his own name by someone who was known to have had no links with the apostles. In spite of this, the gospel was immediately accepted as an authoritative source, and was used as such by Matthew and Luke. Within a hundred years the myth that the author of the gospel was John Mark, the interpreter of Peter – a myth for which there was no historical foundation – was universally accepted in the church. Such a sequence of events was possible because early Christians were gullible people who believed everything they were told and had no idea of the need for accurate sources or the value of eyewitness evidence. Thus Luke's statement in the preface to his gospel that many others before him had written about Jesus on the basis of eyewitness reports, and that his own book was based on careful research over a long period, should be dismissed as bombastic and exaggerated. Most of Luke's information was either taken from Mark (and therefore unapostolic) or invented by Luke himself. If the previous accounts based on eyewitness tradition to which Luke refers ever existed, they have been lost without trace because the early Christians preferred the unapostolic accounts of Mark and his successors.

Eyewitness Testimony in the Early Church

The striking thing about this scenario is not so much the lack of any historical evidence to support it as the fact that the evidence we have points uniformly in the opposite direction. The works of only four early church storytellers are extant: Matthew, Mark, Luke and John. Only two of these give us any formal clue to their authorial practice, and both emphasize eyewitness testimony. Luke refers, as we have just mentioned, to the tradition handed down by the original eyewitnesses and ministers of the word. John 19:35 (with reference to the water and the blood that flowed from Jesus' side on the cross) states that 'the one who has seen has borne witness and his testimony is true and he knows that he is telling the truth so that you too may believe'. John 21:24 (with reference either to the events of chapter 21 or to the gospel as a whole) refers to 'the disciple whom Jesus loved' as 'the disciple who testifies to these things and wrote them, and we know that his testimony is true'. Irrespective of whether or not these statements are regarded as reliable, the assumption behind them is that eyewitness testimony is important to the readers, and that authors must take this into account if they are to gain credibility.

We find the same concern for the handing on of reliable tradition elsewhere in the New Testament. Paul handed on to the church in Corinth traditions he had received about the teaching of Jesus (1 Cor. 7:10, 12, 25), about the Lord's Supper (1 Cor. 11:23–26) and about the resurrection (I Cor: 15.1–11). The resurrection tradition included appearances of Jesus to people personally known to Paul. 2 Timothy 2:2 refers in similar terms to the handing down of tradition through 'reliable people'. Apostolic tradition was widely available in the early church. Peter and the other apostles travelled extensively along with their wives (1 Cor: 9.5), and 2 Peter 1: 16–18, whatever view we take of the letter's provenance, suggests that the church expected reminiscences of Jesus to form part of their teaching.

The emphasis on eyewitness testimony continues in the post-apostolic age. Irenaeus refers to Clement, the bishop of Rome at the end of the first century, as one who 'had seen the blessed apostles and had associated with them, and had the preaching of the apostles still echoing in his ears, and their tradition before his eyes', and asserts that in Clement's time there were still many alive who had received instruction from the apostles.[16] In Irenaeus' opinion the reliability of the tradition had been safeguarded by a properly constituted succession of bishops.[17] He reminds Florinus of how when they were young they both sat at the feet of Bishop Polycarp, and how he still remembers the place where Polycarp sat as he talked to the people about his association with the apostle John and with others who had seen the Lord, how he related from memory their words and the things they told about the Lord, his teaching and his miracles.[18] But Irenaeus also records non-episcopal traditions that purported to come from the apostles at second or third hand. He refers to the reminiscences of 'the elders who had seen John the Lord's disciple', of 'the elders, disciples of the apostles', and even, in one case, of 'an elder who had heard from those who had seen the apostles and from their disciples'.[19] Thus Irenaeus continued, towards the end of the second century, to echo the earlier preference of Papias for the 'living and abiding voice' of those who had heard the teaching of the original eyewitnesses.[20]

We need not assume that the faith of Papias and Irenaeus in these second-hand traditions was always justified. The information that came to them through these channels was of mixed quality, indicating that a living and abiding voice might be more or less impaired with the passage of time. What is striking, however, is the concern, one might almost say the obsession, of some leading figures in the early church for living contact with the apostles, which is in total contrast with the modern theory that early Christians were not bothered whether tradition was apostolic or not.

It is true that the respect for tradition of Paul, Papias and Irenaeus was not universally shared. Paul's letters represent a running battle with rival teachers whose approach to authority differed from his; Papias contrasts his love of apostolic tradition with the attitude of 'the many' who valued verbosity above authenticity; and the apocryphal gospels bear witness to the fluency with which sayings of Jesus could be invented. There was a diversity of approach to tradition in the early church. But it is precisely this diversity that modern critical orthodoxy fails to recognize. It is commonly assumed that all records of the ministry of Jesus based on first-hand evidence have vanished. The only records that remain are those of Mark and his successors, which were known from the beginning to have no apostolic authority and to be based on third- and fourth-hand reports that were circulating in the churches. This monochrome picture is not based on historical evidence, but is a logical requirement to make the modern under-standing of the gospels plausible. To adapt a phrase of William Wrede's, the theory of early church gullibility belongs to the history of dogma.

A Colonial Mentality

It is, perhaps, no coincidence that this way of thinking about the early church arose in the heyday of western imperialism. It was common in the nineteenth and early twentieth centuries to regard Western European culture as superior to all other cultures, whether of the past or of the present. In his book, *No Full Stops in India*, Mark Tully chronicles what he sees as the harmful effects on Indian life and culture of the assumptions of Western superiority. He records that in 1835 the Governor-General of India, Lord Bentinck, ruled that 'the great object of the British Government ought to be the promotion of European literature and science', and directed that all funds available for education should be 'henceforth employed in imparting to the native population knowledge of English literature and science through the medium of the English language'.[21] A similar attitude was rife in the church. In 1910 a young Indian, V.S. Azariah, gave a passionate address to the World Missionary Conference in Edinburgh. He pleaded that the foreign missionary should be to his fellow-Christians 'not a lord and master but a brother and a friend.'[22] It is hard for us in the 1990s to understand the furore created when Azariah was consecrated as bishop in 1912, or the attitude of the missionaries who wrote that they were not willing to serve under an Indian bishop.[23] But all this is understandable in the light of the popular assumption in those days of the innate superiority of modern European culture.

It was natural that the attitudes of society as a whole should be reflected in contemporary New Testament scholarship. D.F. Strauss in his *Life of Jesus* characterized the early church as 'a Church of Orientals, for the most part uneducated people, which consequently was able to adopt and express those ideas only in concrete ways of fantasy, as pictures and as stories, not in the abstract form of rational understanding or concepts'.[24] In Strauss's view the inability of early Christians to think properly was due not only to their lack of education; it was also due to the fact that they were Orientals. Wrede attributes the same inability more to chronology than to topography: it would be most improbable for Mark to have thought historically because he was 'a fairly unsophisticated author of ancient times'.[25] The implication is that Mark's historical ineptitude was typical of the first-century world in which he lived.

Schmidt betrays the influence of a similar cultural arrogance when he dismisses Mark as an unsophisticated, clumsy redactor, who recorded blatant contradictions without having the intelligence to realize what he was doing. The contemptuous appraisal of Mark by so many scholars of that period as an author incapable of elementary historical thinking reflects the attitude of classical Western imperialism. Indeed, it would not be too much to say that those approaches to the study of the gospels which still at the end of the twentieth century trace their pedigree back to Wrede and Schmidt represent one of the last bastions of the colonial mentality.

An Alternative View

The failure of Schmidt to provide logically sound arguments to establish his thesis does not, of course, establish the truth of any other thesis. But there are strong arguments for accepting the main alternative: the early church tradition linking Mark with the apostle Peter. In his *Ecclesiastical History* Eusebius quotes from a work by Bishop Papias (c. 60 – c. 130) who in turn is quoting the words of 'the Elder' – presumably John the Elder, who was one of Papias' main informants.[26]

> And this is what the Elder said. Mark was Peter's interpreter, and he wrote down accurately, but not in order, what he remembered of the words and deeds of the Lord. For he was not a hearer or disciple of the Lord, but at a later stage, as I said, of Peter. Peter used to give his teaching in response to the needs of the people, not with a view to making a collection of the sayings of the Lord. So Mark did nothing wrong in writing some things down in this way as he remembered them; for his one concern was not to leave out anything he had heard and not to make any false statement in recording it.[27]

There are several points to note about this tradition:

i)   The Elder is not seeking to establish Mark's authorship of the gospel, but presupposes it as an agreed fact. The point at issue is not the fact of Mark's authorship, but its quality.

ii)   The Elder seems to be defending Mark against the charge of lack of order.

iii)   His reply to this charge is that Mark was not himself an eyewitness, but was dependent on the teaching of Peter. Peter's teaching was not systematic but occasional: sermons, addresses and anecdotes to suit the needs of the community. Since Mark's aim was to reproduce Peter's teaching as faithfully as possible, he reproduced not only its content but also its style.

We can only guess the background to this charge – whether Mark's lack of order was being contrasted with the systematic teaching in Matthew or the chronological detail in John. Nor should we press the statement that Mark omitted nothing and misrepresented nothing: such a statement, as Martin Hengel says, was a stereotyped formula in the ancient world.[28] What is significant is that, in the time of the Elder John (whom Hengel reckons to have flourished towards the end of the first century)[29] Mark's gospel was already a well-known work that was being compared with the other gospels.

The title of the gospel is 'the gospel according to Mark'. Hengel has argued strongly that the titles of the gospels belonged to them from the beginning. He points out that these titles are undisputed from an early age (which would not have been the case had they been published anonymously) and suggests that the widespread practice among early Christian communities of sharing important documents with other churches would have necessitated titles.[30] The identification of the author of the second gospel as Mark, the assistant of Simon Peter, is not peculiar to Papias but a unanimous tradition of the early church. For example, Justin refers to the story of Jesus coining the names Peter and Boanerges as having been written in Peter's reminiscences.[31] Such an early and universal tradition should not be rejected unless there are overwhelming reasons for doing so.

The usual grounds for rejecting this tradition are internal: the nature of the material in the gospels is such, we are told, that a long period of community tradition must have elapsed to shape it into its present form. In this connection it is important to note what Papias says. Peter, according to the Papias tradition, did not teach systematically but to meet needs (πρὸς τὰς χρείας). Papias here agrees with the modern advocates of community tradition on one important point: that the gospels record the story of Jesus as it was taught in the early Christian communities to meet the needs of those communities. The point at issue is whether, in the community to which Mark belonged, this teaching was being given by Peter or by otherwise unknown preachers and storytellers.

One of the clearest statements of the community-tradition hypothesis is D.E. Nineham's article, 'Eyewitness Testimony and the Gospel Tradition.'[32] The article was written nearly forty years ago, and is concerned with form criticism in its classical guise. But it is still valuable, because it dates from a time when, at least in British scholarship, the Papias tradition was widely accepted,[33] and the case for its rejection had to be argued rather than, as is common today, simply presupposed. Nineham begins by spelling out the characteristics of community tradition on the one hand and eyewitness testimony on the other. Community tradition, he suggests, is marked by the formal, stereotyped character of the sections, the absence of particular individual details and the conventional character of the connecting summaries. The characteristics we should expect in eyewitness testimony, on the other hand, are knowledge of the particular, inclusion of the merely memorable as opposed to the edifying, exact biographical and topographical precision and the like. It is the absence of these latter features that Nineham regards as the essential evidence for the form-critical approach.[34]

Two comments are appropriate. The first is that Mark's gospel provides examples of both the above categories – some stories contain a wealth of vivid detail and others very little. Therefore, if Nineham's distinction were sound, it would require us to attribute the material in Mark to a variety of sources. This is in fact what Vincent Taylor does in his commentary. Taylor divides the groups of narratives in Mark into three categories: groupings made by Mark himself; groupings taken over by Mark as fixed cycles of oral tradition; and groups of narratives based on personal testimony, probably that of Peter. The criterion for inclusion in the third category is the presence of the kind of vivid detail that Nineham defines as characteristic of eyewitness testimony.[35]

However, Nineham rejects Taylor's position. He points out that vivid details are regarded by some scholars, such as Dibelius, as signs of the lateness of the material – as additions made to give verisimilitude or to make a theological point – and that the apocryphal gospels are the richest in vivid touches and circumstantial detail.[36] He accordingly concludes, in his commentary on Mark, that 'all' of Mark's material 'without exception seems to bear the characteristic marks of community tradition.'[37] But there seems little point in listing the features that distinguish community tradition from eyewitness tradition and then going on to say that the factors characteristic of eyewitness tradition are equally characteristic of community tradition. It appears that there is no way Mark could possibly have told his stories without revealing the marks of community tradition to a critic determined to discover them.

The second comment on Nineham's thesis is that the distinction between community tradition and eyewitness tradition is a false one. The eyewitnesses were part of the community. According to the early church fathers, Peter settled at Rome – and if he did not settle there, he settled somewhere else. Even Paul, the most peripatetic of all preachers, spent a year and a half at Corinth, three years at Ephesus and at least two years at Rome. While an apostle lived in a Christian community, he would help to form the tradition of that community. It is surely too much to believe that any Christian community would continue to rely for its knowledge of Jesus on local storytellers when Peter was sitting in their midst.

We may take, for example, the story of Jesus blessing the children in Mark 10:13–16, a story that is not linked to any specific time or place. We may suppose, for the sake of argument, that this story was told mainly in connection with infant baptism and reached its present stylized form through frequent repetition in that context. If there was an infant baptism in Rome during Peter's time there, who would be more likely to tell the story than Peter? And Peter, telling the story for the fiftieth time, would be as likely to stylize it as any other storyteller. Most men (and preachers in particular) have a fund of favourite stories which they repeat in a more or less standard form whenever they get the opportunity; and Peter was a man as well as an apostle. If we are to assume that those who handed on community tradition could tell a story in any way they wanted – adding vivid details here and removing them there – there are no grounds for the assumption that an eyewitness telling the same story in the same community could have told it only in the unique form that twentieth-century scholars have defined as characteristic of eyewitness testimony.

According to Nineham, 'all, or practically all, the material in Mark seems to be of the **pericope** form and so presumably has passed through the formalizing process of community tradition.'[38] Now it may be true that anyone who repeatedly tells detached stories, as the apostle Peter must have done, is subject to a 'formalizing process'. But this would not prevent his stories from being at the same time eyewitness stories that reflected his own personality. It would not mean that his stories were cast in what Nineham calls 'the stereotyped, impersonal form of community tradition'.[39] What is the meaning of 'impersonal tradition'? What Christian community ever has been or ever could be impersonal? One gets the impression that for some critics early Christians were not real people but clones, artificially reproduced in a form-critical laboratory. Tradition is shaped by individuals, and where Christian communities contained eyewitnesses, as many of them would, those eyewitnesses would play a decisive role in both framing and handing down the tradition. At the same time, they would tell stories in the same style as the storytellers who were not eyewitnesses, and would be as liable as they to any formalizing process that was in the air. As John Wenham says:

> There may well be something in the idea that stories gain a certain smoothness, conciseness and impact through frequent repetition. But this is at least as true of the stories of a single eyewitness in the course of a lifetime of itinerant preaching as it is of a succession of preachers borrowing material from their predecessors.[40]

According to Nineham, eyewitness testimony can have played only a minor role in the formation of early church tradition. He asks 'What

Sitz im Leben can be suggested for the process whereby personal testimony intervened in, and modified, the development of the community tradition?'[41]

Nineham's choice of language (limiting the role of the eyewitnesses to intervention and modification) implies a scenario such as the following. In a typical early Christian community storytellers would tell and retell stories that they had received, remodelled or invented. From time to time an eyewitness would appear, rather like a quality control inspector; he would tell them where their stories were wrong, force them to make alterations and then move on elsewhere.

Such a picture does not carry conviction. But this is not because eyewitnesses played an insignificant role in the early church, as Nineham believes. It is because their role was not limited to intervention and modification of the tradition. They were its primary creators and transmitters.

There are three main approaches to the question of Mark's sources. Some scholars accept the early church tradition linking Mark and Peter, and believe that the bulk of Mark's gospel is based on first-hand acquaintance with Peter's teaching. Some scholars totally reject this tradition and believe that Mark had no direct contact with eyewitnesses but relied entirely on the local Christian community. A third group try to strike a compromise, accepting both the general soundness of the argument for community tradition and the strength of the testimony of the early church. Vincent Taylor's commentary is a classic example of this third approach, which was popular in Britain around the middle of the twentieth century. The great problem with it is the question raised by Nineham: why, if Mark had access to Peter's reminiscences, did he not regularly prefer them to community traditions?[42]

Advocates of the compromise approach agree with the form critics that stories told in a conventional way cannot derive directly from Peter. They are therefore forced to believe that Mark, having available to him a fund of vivid stories direct from the lips of Peter, chose instead for the most part to record less vivid stories drawn from the community. This seems incomprehensible. It appears that we must choose between the first two views. *Either* Mark's gospel is based mainly on the teaching of Peter *or* it is based mainly (or entirely) on community tradition.

If we accept the link with Peter, the variations in Mark's gospel can be attributed to two causes: the deliberate choice of Mark to relate some stories in more detail than others; and the variation in Peter's own memory and teaching. On this theory, Peter would sometimes remember an event or a piece of teaching in vivid detail, including the scenery, the time and the place. At other times he would remember the event or the teaching itself but not the background details. This would be particularly true of teaching that Jesus had repeated on various occasions. In some cases the form of Peter's storytelling could have become stylized, as a result of his many years' experience of telling the same stories for the edification of Christian communities. As to the course of Jesus' ministry, he would remember the main events and their sequence, but not the exact time and place of every occurrence within that sequence. Mark was then faced with the need to condense all this information into a small compass. He chose to do this by recording some events in great detail, as he had heard Peter describe them, and some events more briefly, either because Peter used to tell them more briefly or to save space for other items. For the many periods of Jesus' ministry that he was forced to leave unreported he relied on summary statements. These statements would be composed, in the words of C.E.B. Cranfield, 'on the basis of a general knowledge of the course of the ministry possessed by him as a result of his association with Peter.'[43]

This reconstruction is, of course, hypothetical. But it explains the stylistic variations in Mark in a way that makes sense. If, on the other hand, we follow the modern approach that ties Mark to community tradition, we are faced with many problems. This approach rests on three assumptions, all equally improbable:

i) that the unanimous belief of the early church in a direct link between Mark and Peter is historically worthless.

ii) that early Christians (including the evangelists) were people of low intelligence, who consistently showed no interest in the historical facts of the life of Jesus and no preference for eyewitness testimony.

iii) that the arguments from design, from silence, from contradiction etc., in the form in which they are employed by the advocates of this approach, are sound, logical arguments.

I have concentrated on the third of these assumptions, while recognizing that one cannot establish a positive by a negative. The direction of logical weaknesses in Schmidt's arguments does not disprove Schmidt's position, and indeed cannot do so, since his position is a dogmatic one. Nor can it establish the alternative position linking Mark and Peter. What it does achieve is to call into question the popular opinion that Schmidt has 'demonstrated' his thesis. If one of the foundation pillars of modern critical orthodoxy has feet not of concrete but of clay, this is bound to have implications for the theories built upon that foundation.

Notes

1   Rudolf Bultmann in R. Bultmann and Karl Kundsin, *Form Criticism* tr. Frederick C. Grant (Harper, New York 1962) 25.
2   Schmidt, *Rahmen* 192. This passage was discussed in Chapter Six pp.73f.
3   William R. Telford, *The Interpretation of Mark* (Edinburgh, T & T Clark 1995²) 13. Telford refers to D.O. Via Jr., J.R. Donahue and E. Güttgemanns as representative of this sceptical approach to scissors-and-paste criticism.
4   Schmidt, *Rahmen* 33.
5   Ibid. 303.
6   Telford, *Interpretation* 40.
7   Ibid. 5 quoted in Introduction p. 4.
8   Martin Hengel, *Studies in the Gospel of Mark* tr. John Bowden (SCM Press, London 1985) 52.
9   James M. Robinson, *A New Quest of the Historical Jesus* (SCM Press, London 1959) 35–7.
10   Schmidt's *Rahmen* and M. Dibelius, *Die Formgeschichte des Evangeliums* were both published in 1919. R. Bultmann, *Die Geschichte der Synoptischen Tradition* was published in 1921.
11   In the light of the attempt of some form critics to find the *Sitz im Leben* of New Testament pericopes *either* in preaching *or* in worship, it is interesting to note that Schmidt has a unitary approach:

> When the Christian communities gathered for worship, and in gatherings arranged by an evangelist to win new Christians, the short self-contained accounts of specific deeds and words of Jesus had a part to play. These two types of gathering need not be strictly distinguished from each other; community gatherings were not completely exclusive, and when interested outsiders took part in them, they promoted the cause of mission by that very fact (*Rahmen* 304).

12   cf. the quotation from R. Bultmann on p. 157.
13   According to Schmidt, the individual stories in the pre-Markan tradition were grouped together on a practical basis, in the light of a number of practical considerations that are not always immediately obvious, because they are bound up with the history of early Christianity and its various religious, apologetic and missionary concerns (*Rahmen* 317). Schmidt here recognizes a theological element in Mark, but on the whole sees him as reactive rather than proactive.
14   cf. Telford, *Interpretation* 13: 'Given the often atomistic nature of a strict form- and redaction-critical procedure, and given the complexity revealed by its results in a text once considered simple, it is not surprising that there has been a call for a more holistic approach to the Gospel. The hermeneutical task should begin

with a literary analysis unencumbered with historical suppositions, its propo-
nents claim, and this is surely correct.' Telford points out that this apparent
'flight from history' has been criticized by other scholars, but believes it has
brought a rich new dimension to Markan studies.

15 For further discussion of this point see *Seven Pillories* 12f.
16 Irenaeus, A.H. 3.3.2–3.
17 Ibid. 3.3.1.
18 Eusebius, H.E. 5.20.5–7.
19 Irenaeus, A.H. 5.33.3; 5.36.2; 4.27.1.
20 Papias in Eusebius H.E. 3.39.4.
21 Mark Tully, *No Full Stops in India* (Penguin Books, London 1991) 7.
22 Carol Graham, *Azariah of Dornakal* (SCM Press, London 1946) 39.
23 Ibid. 37.
24 D.F. Strauss, *Das Leben Jesu, kritisch bearbeitet* as translated in W.G. Kümmel,
    The New Testament: The History of the Investigation of its Problems tr. S. McLean
    Gilmour & Howard C. Kee (SCM Press, London 1972) 120.
25 Wrede, *Secret* 132 (E), 132 (G).
26 Opinions differ as to whether 'John the Elder' was another way of referring to
    John the apostle, or whether, as Eusebius believed, Papias was referring to two
    separate people both called John.
27 Eusebius H.E. 3.39.15.
28 Hengel, *Studies* 49.
29 Ibid. 47.
30 Martin Hengel, 'The Titles of the Gospels and the Gospel of Mark' in *Studies*
    64–84.
31 Justin, *Dialogue with Trypho* 106.3. The Greek text of this passage can be found
    in Hengel, *Studies* 155 n. 69. The name-coining is referred to in Mark 3:16f.
32 Dennis E. Nineham, 'Eyewitness Testimony and the Gospel Tradition' in *JTS*
    ns. IX (1958) – Part I pp.13–25; Part II pp.243–52.
33 The two British commentaries on the Greek text of Mark that appeared around
    that time both support the Papias tradition. Vincent Taylor states that 'the
    Papias tradition has been widely accepted, and with good reason' (V. Taylor,
    The Gospel according to St. Mark [Macmillan, London 1952] 3). C.E.B. Cran-
    field writes: 'the unanimous tradition of the early Church that the author of the
    gospel was Mark, the associate of Peter, is not open to serious doubt.' (C.E.B.
    Cranfield, *The Gospel according to St. Mark* [Cambridge University Press,
    Cambridge 1959] 5).
34 Nineham, *Testimony* 13.
35 Taylor, *Mark* 102.
36 Nineham, *Testimony* 22.
37 D.E. Nineham, *Saint Mark* (Penguin Books, Harmondsworth 1963) 27.
38 Nineham, *Testimony* 20.
39 Ibid. 243. Cf. the reference on p.22 to 'the impersonal tradition of the
    community'.
40 John Wenham, *Redating Matthew, Mark and Luke* (Hodder & Stoughton,
    London 1991) 181.
41 Nineham, *Testimony* 16.
42 Ibid. 22.
43 Cranfield, *Mark* 18.

Index